OVERCOMING ANGER AND IRRITABILITY

A self-help guide using
Cognitive Behavioral Techniques

WILLIAM DAVIES

ROBINSON
London

Constable & Robinson Ltd
3 The Lanchesters
162 Fulham Palace Road
London W6 9ER
www.constablerobinson.com

First published in the UK by Robinson,
an imprint of Constable & Robinson Ltd, 2000

A copy of the British Library Cataloguing in
Publication Data is available from the British Library.

Important Note

This book is not intended as a substitute for medical advice or treatment.
Any person with a condition requiring medical attention should consult
a qualified medical practitioner or suitable therapist.

ISBN 978-1-85487-595-2

Printed and bound in the EU

Table of contents

Acknowledgements

Reading through previous Acknowledgements contained in books in this series I see that the form is to thank all the wonderful people that have written about and researched Cognitive Therapy. Quite right too, I hope that is taken as read. More immediately, however, I would like to thank Amy and Helen for the work they put in to typing this book at very short notice, under great pressure, and with very little irritation! (One or two assertive comments perhaps, but probably well justified!) Also to Paul Gilbert for pushing forward what he terms my 'approachable writing style' and, just as much, to the publishers for creating a series that is so relevant and important that it makes one enthusiastic to write for it. Finally, although I can't imagine they will ever read this, an acknowledgement to 'Danny and Vicky' who feature in one of the many case studies and who may well be recognised for the well-known characters they are. A special word of thanks to them for the endless entertainment they provide, and of reassurance that their inclusion is not yet another dig at them, but is simply intended to create an entirely non-malicious smile in the reader.

Introduction

Why a cognitive behavioral approach?

Over the past two or three decades, there has been something of a revolution in the field of psychological treatment. Freud and his followers had a major impact on the way in which psychological therapy was conceptualized, and psychoanalysis and psychodynamic psychotherapy dominated the field for the first half of this century. So, long-term treatments were offered which were designed to uncover the childhood roots of personal problems – offered, that is, to those who could afford it. There was some attempt by a few health service practitioners with a public conscience to modify this form of treatment (by, for example, offering short-term treatment or group therapy), but the demand for help was so great that this had little impact. Also, whilst numerous case histories can be found of people who are convinced that psychotherapy did help them, practitioners of this form of therapy showed remarkably little interest in demonstrating that what they were offering their patients was, in fact, helpful.

As a reaction to the exclusivity of psychodynamic therapies and the slender evidence for its usefulness, in the 1950s and 1960s a set of techniques was developed, broadly collectively termed 'behavior therapy'. These techniques shared two basic features. First, they aimed to remove symptoms (such as anxiety) by dealing with those symptoms themselves, rather than their deep-seated underlying historical causes. Second, they were techniques, loosely related to what laboratory psychologists were finding out about the mechanisms of learning, which were formulated in testable terms. Indeed, practitioners of behavior therapy were committed to using techniques of proven value or, at worst, of a form which could potentially be put to the test. The area where these techniques proved of most value was in the treatment of anxiety disorders, especially specific phobias (such as fear of animals or heights) and agoraphobia, both notoriously difficult to treat using conventional psychotherapies.

After an initial flush of enthusiasm, discontent with behavior therapy grew. There were a number of reasons for this, an important one of which was the fact that behavior therapy did not deal with the internal thoughts which were so obviously central to the distress that patients were experiencing. In this context, the fact that behavior therapy proved so inadequate when it came to the treatment of depression highlighted the need for major revision. In the late 1960s and early 1970s a treatment was developed specifically for depression called 'cognitive therapy'. The pioneer in this enterprise was an American psychiatrist, Professor Aaron T. Beck, who developed a theory of depression which emphasized the importance of people's depressed styles of thinking. He also specified a new form of therapy. It would not be an exaggeration to say that Beck's work has changed the nature of psychotherapy, not just for depression but for a range of psychological problems.

In recent years the cognitive techniques introduced by Beck have been merged with the techniques developed earlier by the behavior therapists to produce a body of theory and practice which has come to be known as 'cognitive behavior therapy'. There are two main reasons why this form of treatment has come to be so important within the field of psychotherapy. First, cognitive therapy for depression, as originally described by Beck and developed by his successors, has been subjected to the strictest scientific testing; and it has been found to be a highly successful treatment for a significant proportion of cases of depression. Not only has it proved to be as effective as the best alternative treatments (except in the most severe cases, where medication is required), but some studies suggest that people treated successfully with cognitive behavior therapy are less likely to experience a later recurrence of their depression than people treated successfully with other forms of therapy (such as antidepressant medication). Second, it has become clear that specific patterns of thinking are associated with a range of psychological problems and that treatments which deal with these styles of thinking are highly effective. So, specific cognitive behavioral treatments have been developed for anxiety disorders, like panic disorder, generalized anxiety disorder, specific phobias and social phobia, obsessive compulsive disorders, and hypochondriasis (health anxiety), as well as for other conditions such as compulsive gambling, alcohol and drug addiction, and eating disorders like bulimia nervosa and binge-eating disorder. Indeed, cognitive behavioral techniques have a wide application beyond the narrow categories of psychological disorders: they have been applied effectively, for example, to helping people with low self-esteem and those with marital difficulties.

At any one time almost 10 per cent of the general population is suffering from depression, and more than 10 per cent has one or other of the anxiety disorders. Many others have a range of psychological problems and personal difficulties. It is of the greatest importance that treatments of proven effectiveness are developed. However, even when the armoury of therapies is, as it were, full, there remains a very great problem – namely that the delivery of treatment is expensive and the resources are not going to be available evermore. Whilst this shortfall could be met by lots of people helping themselves, commonly the natural inclination to make oneself feel better in the present is to do precisely those things which perpetuate or even exacerbate one's problems. For example, the person with agoraphobia will stay at home to prevent the possibility of an anxiety attack; and the person with bulimia nervosa will avoid eating all potentially fattening foods. Whilst such strategies might resolve some immediate crisis, they leave the underlying problem intact and provide no real help in dealing with future difficulties.

So, there is a twin problem here: although effective treatments have been developed, they are not widely available;

and when people try to help themselves they often make matters worse. In recent years the community of cognitive behavior therapists have responded to this situation. What they have done is to take the principles and techniques of specific cognitive behavior therapies for particular problems and represent them in self-help manuals. These manuals specify a systematic program of treatment which the individual sufferer is advised to work through to overcome their difficulties. In this way, the cognitive behavioral therapeutic techniques of proven value are being made available on the widest possible basis.

Self-help manuals are never going to replace therapists. Many people will need individual treatment from a qualified therapist. It is also the case that, despite the widespread success of cognitive behavioral therapy, some people will not respond to it and will need one of the other treatments available. Nevertheless, although research on the use of cognitive behavioral self-help manuals is at an early stage, the work done to date indicates that for a very great many people such a manual will prove sufficient for them to overcome their problems without professional help.

Many people suffer silently and secretly for years. Sometimes appropriate help is not forthcoming despite their efforts to find it. Sometimes they feel too ashamed or guilty to reveal their problems to anyone. For many of these people the cognitive behavioral self-help manuals will provide a lifeline to recovery and a better future.

Professor Peter Cooper
The University of Reading

PART ONE

Understanding
What Happens

1

What are irritability and anger?

We are probably right to put irritability and anger together because they are so often associated with each other. Nevertheless they are somewhat different. Consider the following stories:

I was in the pub one evening with a couple of friends, just sitting near the back door to the pub, talking. It was a November evening and it was quite cold outside. Somebody came through the back door and left it just a little open so that I had to get up and close it. I didn't mind too much. About a quarter of an hour later somebody else came in and did the same thing, didn't quite close the door properly. So I got up again and closed it. A little while later a third person did the same thing. I closed the door, but gave him a good hard stare. Mind you, I don't think he noticed because he was walking to the bar by that time so I was staring at the back of his head. It happened a fourth time a bit later on – the thing is, the self-closing mechanism on the door had broken. Anyway, this time I said to the bloke who'd come in, 'Don't you think you should close the door behind you when you come in?' He just looked at me as though I was some kind of oddball and went and ordered himself a drink. It was when the fifth person came in that I really went to town on him. By this time I had sunk probably four or five pints. He did exactly the same as all the others, left the door just slightly open. The thing that really got me about it was that they don't seem to care, they just seem so intent on getting their own drinks inside them that they don't give a damn about anybody else in the pub. Anyway, something snapped in me. I didn't actually hit the bloke but I jumped up, started shouting and swearing at him, jabbing my finger in his chest and generally calling him all the names under the sun. He was only a small bloke. And the funny thing was he had only done exactly the same thing as the first one. Simply left the door a little open.

Compare that story, told by a 28-year-old man, Steve, with the following one from David, aged 45.

It was a Wednesday evening and four of us went down to town for a meal in an Indian restaurant. That's me, my wife and the two kids. Anyway, we parked the car in a back street, it must have been about eight o'clock in the evening, walked round to the restaurant and had a very good meal. It was the first time we'd been there, we were all on good form, had a good laugh and a joke about everything, even at how thick and new the carpets were, and altogether had a thoroughly good time. Anyway, about half-past nine or ten o'clock, we'd just turned the corner of the street we'd parked the car in when we heard an almighty crash and the sound of breaking glass. Except it hardly sounded like glass, it was a stronger, louder sound than that. We looked down the street, and there was some bloke with his head stuck through the passenger window of our car, and another bloke standing by him. I didn't grasp what was happening for a moment; then I realized that the sound we had heard was the window glass breaking, and these two were in the process of stealing the stereo from my car. Anyway, I felt that mixture of stuff that courses through your body when these things happen, shouted but not very loud, and set off after these two. One bloke saw me after a couple of seconds and just ran off. That left the guy with his head still through the window, engrossed in prising my hi-fi out of the car. He still had his head through the window when I got there. I just grabbed hold of him and pulled him out – I didn't care if his head caught on the bits of broken glass or not – and manhandled him, not at all gently, on to the floor. By this time my wife was there and telling me to take it easy, and one of the kids had already got his mobile phone out and was dialling for the police. The lad I'd got out of the car was never more than sixteen, but I just had him on the floor and could cheerfully have throttled him. What did they think they were doing, just thinking they could go up to somebody else's property and take it? Anyway, I just sat astride

*him, threatening him and telling him what a useless
piece of machinery he was until the police came. Half
a dozen people must have gone past us during all that,
but I couldn't care less. When the police arrived they
did at least seem to take my side, took all the details
and took him off in their car.*

Which of those two stories would you say illustrated irritability and which one anger? To my mind, irritability is shown in the first one and anger in the second. But there is another question, perhaps a more important one, posed by these two examples, and that is: which of the two men was justified in his reaction? Or, if you think that both were justified in their reactions, which was *more* justified?

The 'justified?' test

Personally, I would say the man in the second example was more justified: the man who caught somebody trying to steal his stereo. But maybe I say that because I have been in pretty much the same situation, coming back to the car after a nice meal out, only to find the window broken and the stereo gone. And I must say, if I had been able to get hold of the person who had done it, just at that instant I don't know what I would have done to him. So I feel that I can't really blame David.

On the other hand, I have also inadvertently left a door open and probably irritated somebody thereby – especially if I was the fifth person to have done so that evening. So I would say that perhaps the guy who reacted aggressively in that scene was a bit over-aggressive. Maybe in an ideal world Steve could have toned it down a bit and simply asked persons two, three and four to shut the door after them. But there again, he'd got a few drinks inside him, so possibly his inhibitions were weakened a bit by the time person number five came in. And also he said that customer five was a small bloke, so perhaps that had a bearing on events too.

One of the main judgements we make whenever we see someone behaving in an aggressive or hostile way is whether they are *justified* in doing so. If we consider that they are justified, then we probably won't describe that person as irritable; we reserve the term 'irritable' for people who are hostile, angry or aggressive *without good cause*. If we think the person is justified in being angry or aggressive, then we tend to see nothing wrong with that. So, if we see David as justified in his anger, we probably won't blame him for pinning the thief to the ground until the police arrive. We might see that as a proportionate response. If, on the other hand, he had started banging the 16-year-old's head up and down on the pavement while loudly cursing him, we might have seen that as disproportionate and unjustified.

So, if we really want a definition of irritability it will be something along the lines of: *an unjustified negative response to a situation*. Unjustified in whose eyes? In ours, of course. And therein lies a problem, because everybody has a different judgement as to what is justified and what isn't. What is more, sometimes our judgement goes a little hazy. I can still remember the first time I saw the film *One Flew*

Over the Cuckoo's Nest, in which Nurse Ratchet torments a group of mentally ill patients led by Jack Nicholson. Certainly the patients were full of antipathy towards Nurse Ratchet after about an hour of the film, but not half as much as the audience. At this point, after Nurse Ratchet's particularly savage treatment of one of the patients, Jack Nicholson could stand it no longer, grabbed hold of her, had her on the floor and was throttling the life out of her. Half the audience in the cinema was on its feet, shouting encouragement and just hoping he would finish the job before the two male nurses rushing to Ms Ratchet's assistance could get there. He didn't, the authorities got the better of him, and we all trudged unhappily out of the cinema.

Even though Nurse Ratchet's behavior was extreme, perhaps Jack Nicholson's response was somewhat disproportionate. Of course, in a case like this our judgement is clouded by the events being on the silver screen rather than in reality. But this 'temporary clouding of judgement' is exactly the problem; because, unfortunately, it happens not just on the silver screen but in real life as well. On those occasions we get repeatedly remorseful and self-critical. We say we 'over-reacted' or 'don't know what got hold of us'. We feel that our response was out of all proportion to the event; it was not *justified*.

These are themes that will run throughout this book. How do we get ourselves always – or nearly always – to respond to negative events in a way that is *in proportion* to them? In a way that we, and others, would say is *justified*?

It is worth lingering a little on these questions of definition. The word 'irritability' implies a minor kind of response on the part of the irritable person, probably verbal, usually not physically aggressive. Even so, we tend to react against irritable people because we think that their response is not justified. Anger, on the other hand, might lead to a much more forceful response. The man who pinned the thief to the floor was angry. Nevertheless, we don't necessarily react against people who are being angry, so long as we see their anger as justified.

In fact, we sometimes like to see people getting angry, so long as they are on our side. Margaret Thatcher was often referred to as 'handbagging' her counterparts from other European countries in order to stick up for those in Britain perceived as their rights. I, for one, never heard many people complaining about that at the time. Her successor John Major, on the other hand, was painted as a much more grey character (literally in the case of the satirical *Spitting Image* programme): so grey, in fact, that he would be unlikely to get openly angry with too many people. Whether this perception was accurate is another matter but, accurate or not, it seemed to count against him. What is more, this negative perception of John Major was exacerbated by rumours that he could also be rather irritable in private – a shade on the snappish side when perhaps it wasn't warranted. Again, whether this perception was true is another matter, but it does illustrate the point that what people dislike is not the fact of other people getting angry, it's the fact of other people reacting in a way that is not justified, or out of proportion to the situation.

Anger, irritability and frustration

Just to finish off this chapter, see what you make of the following two stories.

The first was related to me by Anne, a woman of 34, telling me about how she was getting on with her 12-year-old daughter.

The biggest rumpus Rachel and I have had this week was Tuesday evening. Of course, it's half-way through the holidays and she always gets on my nerves in the holidays anyway. But Tuesday was particularly bad because I'd been going on at her all day to tidy her room. It was a terrible mess, she could hardly set foot in it without tripping over something – and it smells when you walk in there, I'm sure she's got some food that's going off buried under all her clothes on the floor. Anyway, I'd been going on at her all day to tidy her room and she just wouldn't do it. There was always something she had to do first. So, it was about seven o'clock in the evening, I was downstairs and Rachel was upstairs. I'd just got back from the shops, I'd only been out five or ten minutes. Anyway, the house was quiet so I thought that maybe Rachel had decided that she'd better do what her mum says and get on with tidying her room. So I went upstairs ready to praise her and tell her what a good girl she was and how pleased I was with her and how much better the room looked and so on. When I got up there I could see that Rachel wasn't in her room and the place looked just as much of a tip as it ever had. Anyway, to cut a long story short, there was Rachel, in the bathroom, sitting in the bath washing her hair. Well, I just flew at her. It was absolutely the last straw. She hasn't lifted a finger to help all holidays, she can't even be bothered to tidy her own room, and there she is sitting in the bath like a little madam washing her hair with my shampoo! I just ranted and raved at her for a good ten or fifteen minutes, just shouting and screaming. All the frustrations of the holidays came out in that time. The poor kid looked absolutely petrified, and as for what the neighbours thought, I've no idea.

Justified? Perhaps not.

And what about this one, in which Paul, 46, told me about his son John, also aged 12?

You see, the thing is, all I've ever tried to do is to do my best for him. And I have learnt the hard way that if you don't pay proper attention to education and schooling then you're the worse off for it as you get older. So I'm always going on at him about how impor-tant it is to pay attention in school and do his home-work properly when he gets home. But he knows better, of course, and he tells me that he can concentrate better doing his homework in front of the television. And I've seen him doing it. He sits there, mouth half open, staring at the screen and just every now and again looking at what he's meant to be doing. And he thinks he's got me fooled doing this. He thinks that I believe he's doing his homework. So anyway, Monday was like that, Tuesday was the same, just the same as any other day, and on Wednesday I told him to show me his books after he'd packed them away and said he'd done all the homework he had to do. And so I was looking at his exercise book, for maths; he was meant to have done twenty sums in it. And he's got all the numbers 1 to 20 down there, and some of them he'd done, though God knows whether they were right or not, but I could see that more than half the sums he was meant to have done he just hadn't. He hadn't even tried to. There were just blank spaces where the answers were meant to be. So I saw red and I just walloped him. He was sitting just opposite from me looking stupid and frightened and I just walloped him. I hit him straight across the face so he all but fell off the chair and I didn't waste my breath on him, I just told him to get straight upstairs to bed. And I've not spoken to him since, and that was three days ago.

Justified? Well, again, maybe not. But it is all too easy to be critical of those two parents, or say that their reactions were out of proportion to what triggered them and therefore were not justified. Sometimes people get to such a pitch that they can no longer tell what's justified and what isn't; and both of those parents described, quite truthfully, genuinely wanting to do the best for their children. Sometimes the level of frustration that builds up is unbearable. This was not the first such incident for either of these parents. Both had tried all sorts of tactics without success. And now they saw themselves still as having no success –

but also having been pushed into doing things they didn't like doing.

SUMMARY

- Irritability and anger take lots of different forms. Both are emotions that most people have felt.
- There's nothing wrong with being angry in itself; sometimes it is clearly justified. It is when we overreact, responding in a way that is out of proportion to the situation, that we lay ourselves open to criticism. And sometimes we ourselves are our harshest critics.
- The very term 'irritability' implies that the reaction is unjustified. It normally suggests that a person is being snappy and bad-tempered when there is no call to be so. As such it fails the 'Justified?' test; people are almost always criticized for being irritable. Again, we may be our harshest critics in this respect.
- There are times when, through frustration or for other reasons, we lose our sense of perspective. It's on those occasions that we find ourselves unable to judge what is justified. And then we see ourselves doing things which we feel are justified *at the time* but which later on – once our true sense of judgement returns – we are horrified that we did.

A final thought

Most of us feel rather critical of irritable and unjustifiably angry people, almost as if they were doing it deliberately to make our lives miserable. And, certainly, it is no fun at all living with an irritable and unjustifiably angry person.

One point that is sometimes forgotten, however, is that neither is it any fun being the irritable and angry person! Many, many people have their lives virtually ruined by their own irritability and anger. So it is *both* for them *and* for those around them that this book is written.

2

What makes us angry?

It is important to know just what makes you angry, because when you come to doing something about it this will be a very important starting point. Clearly, if you know what things make you angry, you can either avoid those things (if possible!) or work out how you would prefer to respond when they happen.

So what kind of things are we looking for? It is said that we are all different, but in fact there tend to be certain themes which produce anger in most people. And remember, we said in Chapter 1 that there is nothing wrong with anger in itself, so long as it is in proportion to the event. What makes us feel bad is when we act out of proportion to what is happening: when we are 'snappy' in the face of no reasonable provocation, or angry in response to something that would normally just mildly irritate most people, or completely 'lose our cool' in response to something that most people would just get somewhat angry about.

Irritants, costs and transgressions

So what makes most of us angry? There are three main categories: irritants, costs and transgressions.

Irritants

The number of *irritants* in life is boundless. I was talking recently to Pam, who said she could no longer stand the way her husband ate. Simply the noise his mouth made in chewing his food drove her round the bend. Moreover, as so often happens, now she had noticed this, she was waiting for it every mealtime; and that made it ten times worse. It had become a symbol for all that was wrong with him (self-centred, greedy) and with their marriage (she saw him as a different type of person from herself).

People sniffing, coughing, blowing their noses can also be irritating. This certainly used to be the case for me. I sometimes run training events where I spend three days with perhaps a dozen people. Occasionally one of that dozen will have a chronic, hacking cough which lasts for the duration of these three days and longer, for all I know. Certainly I used to find that very irritating indeed. A cough can be so loud; and sometimes its owner seemed deliberately to cough just as I was coming out with an extremely good point! So then I'd have to repeat it and the effect was spoilt. (I cured myself of this sensitivity when I realized that, very often, the owner of the cough would have been perfectly entitled to stay at home, off sick, for the three days. I was therefore able to re-interpret his coughing presence as a compliment to myself: evidence that he simply could not bear to miss out on the event. Whether this is actually true or not doesn't really matter to me; I feel it is true – or at least it could be true – and that keeps me satisfied.)

Neighbours are another excellent source of irritation. Apartments and town houses give everybody great scope for irritating each other. When we were first married, my wife and I lived in a house where we could even hear the neighbours turning on and off their electric switches at the wall sockets, as clearly as if they were in the room with us. That in itself hardly counts as an irritant, but there is plenty of potential for serious irritation: loud music, raised voices, banging picture-hooks into walls, do-it-yourself activity, playing ball games in the street (and on *your* garden) and so on and so on. Not infrequently people's lives are made a complete misery by the sheer level of irritation provoked by their neighbours.

Costs

The cost to you of somebody else's behavior may be a literal, financial cost, or it may be a cost in terms of time, or in terms of loss of 'face', or indeed any other loss. The common thread here is that, by virtue of what they do, someone costs you in some way; and that makes you angry. Examples include parents being angry when their children break things (because of the financial cost of replacing them); or your spouse being angry because you have crashed the car (again because of the cost of repairing it, or the increased insurance premiums that result).

Interestingly, these kinds of causes of anger sometimes illustrate a 'hangover' effect. Sue told me how angry she was that her 13-year-old son had broken a mug by dropping it on the kitchen floor accidentally. When I asked her exactly why it was that she had become angry she said, 'Well, it's the cost of replacing these things; he goes around as though money grows on trees, thinks that whatever he breaks will just automatically get replaced.' I found this strange, because Sue was very far from being poor, and was well able to replace a broken mug or two. But she had not always been wealthy; at one time in her life it would have made a significant impact on her finances to have to buy a new mug, and that cast of mind had stayed with her. Old habits die hard. And there is another possible explanation, too; but we will come on to that later.

Judy was telling me how she had taken her 5-year-old daughter to a hospital outpatient clinic. She got there promptly for her 2 p.m. appointment but was not seen until approximately two hours later, 4 p.m. What especially enraged her was that she realized after a while that every single person in the clinic had been given an appointment for 2 p.m., and the clinic was due to run from 2 p.m. to 5 p.m. approximately. Therefore, the hospital authorities had deliberately arranged the session in such a way that some people would be waiting for three hours. The costs to Judy were several, including the loss of time in which she could have been doing some of the many tasks that were pressing on her at home; the necessity to entertain her 5-year-old daughter constantly for two hours to prevent her getting bored and restless; and the loss of face implied by the hospital authority's apparent attitude that it didn't matter if she was kept waiting for one, two or three hours.

Alan, an electrician, was angry because he was asked to do too much at work. His boss asked in a very straightforward way, something like, 'Have you got time to fit in an extra call to a customer who needs their light switches sorting out?' and was quite prepared to take no for an answer; he could always ask another of the electricians. Nevertheless, Alan was still angry because of the cost to him of the request. What was that cost? The way he saw it, he could choose one of two: either he suffered the cost of time, whereby he did an extra job that he couldn't really fit into his schedule; or he suffered the cost of guilt in turning down a straightforward request from his boss. Clearly Alan needed to learn some deep assertiveness techniques, so that he could feel entitled to say 'no' without feeling guilty about it.

I have met a lot of people who get very angry and irritated when their partners contradict them in public. The cost here is usually loss of face – especially when the contradiction implies that the first speaker was telling a lie, even if only a harmless little lie to exaggerate and make more interesting an otherwise boring story. Nigel, however, was driven wild by the very smallness of the contradiction. He gave me the example of an occasion when he and his wife were chatting with friends and he was recounting a story of something that had happened the previous Wednesday. As soon as he uttered the word 'Wednesday' his wife interrupted to say, 'No it wasn't, it was last Tuesday.' It is difficult to imagine that he could be made so angry by the cost of such an interruption: there is, after all, hardly any loss of face involved in mistaking a Tuesday for a Wednesday. Perhaps it was just a case of a simple irritant (having his flow of thought interrupted) – or possibly it was something different: a transgression.

Transgressions

A transgression involves the breaking of a rule. Possibly Nigel held to the rule that husbands and wives don't contradict each other in public – not at all an unusual rule to have. Therefore, when that rule was broken, repeatedly, he got angry, repeatedly.

Another very common rule that good friends and partners have is that confidences should not be broken. In other words, if your partner knows something about you purely by virtue of being your partner, then he or she should not go around telling other people about it. This might include intimate details about your health, your likes and dislikes, or simply something they know about your experiences or opinions which you would not share with anybody except your nearest and dearest. To break such confidences is almost universally viewed as a taboo, a major transgression – and one of the very quickest ways you can get on the wrong side of your partner.

Obviously, the example in Chapter 1 about the man who got angry with the youngster he caught trying to steal his car stereo is also an example of a transgression. In that case the youngster was not just breaking a rule held by the man in question, he was breaking the law: a very formalized transgression.

These three categories are not mutually exclusive: there are many cases that cross the boundaries. For example, if your partner flirts with someone he or she finds attractive, that is normally viewed as a transgression; in other words, it is against the rules for many people. But it also involves a cost – loss of face, the impression that your partner is somehow dissatisfied with you and seeking consolation elsewhere. (Of course, this may not be true; but it is easily and often seen that way.)

Another cross-boundary example was the case of Sue's son, who accidentally dropped a mug on the floor and broke it. Perhaps it was, as his mother claimed, the cost of replacing the mug that made her angry; but, given that she could afford to do that without even noticing the price, that seems rather unlikely. A more probable explanation is that she was angry because he had transgressed an unspoken rule, namely that one takes a reasonable amount of care not to inconvenience others in the household. The 'sheer carelessness' was what made her angry.

SUMMARY

- It is important to know the sort of things which make you angry, because you will use this knowledge to benefit yourself later on.
- Typically, there are three categories of event that make people angry: irritants, costs and transgressions.
- There are plenty of irritants: people leaving doors open repeatedly, neighbours making a noise, even the way people eat or cough.
- Likewise, there are plenty of things that people do that have a cost for us: our children breaking things and the consequent

financial cost; our partners contradicting us and costing us loss of face; having to do things unexpectedly, which costs us time.

- You, like everyone else, will have a set of rules that you expect other people to abide by. When someone breaks one of those rules, it is known as a transgression. When you spot a transgression, or think you have, the chances are you will be angry.
- Some things which make us angry straddle the boundaries between these categories. For example, a child breaking something may make us angry because of the cost involved in replacing it, but also because they have not, in our view, taken sufficient care.

3

Why am I not angry all the time?

It does seem that the world is absolutely crammed full with irritants, people doing things that have costs for us, and people breaking the rules we have made up for ourselves; so how come we are not in a permanent state of anger and rage?

Internal and external inhibitions

Remember Judy, who took her youngster to the outpatient clinic at the hospital and was kept waiting for two hours? She described that event to me as one of the times she has been most angry in her life. There were various factors in the build-up. When she first got there, she saw the waiting room was very crowded, but thought perhaps there were quite a few doctors and nurses working, so that it would soon clear. Gradually she realized that, on the contrary, the queue was moving only very slowly; and when she got talking to some of the others there, she found that every one of them had a 2 p.m. appointment. That caused a major step change in her level of anger, from quite calm to 'pretty angry'. Not 'absolutely boiling', however: that came when, at around 3 p.m., the sole doctor and nurse who were in fact working at the clinic that day stopped to have their afternoon tea. And why shouldn't they? you ask; most of us perhaps take a short break in the afternoon, and they had been working hard. Why not, indeed; but it was the manner of their doing it that provoked Judy. For they sat in the clinic room chatting to each other with the door wide open, so that all the patients could see them having their break – all the mothers (mostly) with their youngsters getting increasingly fretful while doctor and nurse only too visibly maintained their right to have a cup of tea. Not surprisingly, then, by the time Judy took her little girl in to see the doctor she was purple with rage. So did she give the doctor a piece of her mind? No; she didn't say a word about it.

Now, this is amazing on the face of it, because if you talk to Judy now, ten years after that event, she still begins seething at the recollection of it. She was *so angry*. And yet she simply didn't mention it when she got to see the doctor. Why could that be?

The short answer is: because of her *inhibitions*. It's not that Judy is an 'inhibited' kind of person, just that there were inhibitions in action that held her back; some kind of self-control mechanism. We can probably guess the kind of thoughts that were going through her mind – things like: 'If I get on the wrong side of the doctor, will my youngster get the best treatment he is capable of providing?' Judy, indeed, confirms that this is true, that is exactly the thought that was uppermost in her mind. But she also confesses to a secondary inhibition, namely: 'You just don't go around getting angry with doctors.' Rightly or wrongly, she held this as a rule for herself, a rule that held good even when she was so badly treated by a doctor.

That second inhibition ('you don't get angry with doctors') is termed an *internal* inhibition: in other words, it is an inhibition which exists entirely internally, in the mind. There is no external threat, like the police coming to arrest her, which would prevent her from being angry with the doctor – purely an internal rule she had for herself.

What about the first inhibition? The one which said maybe her child wouldn't get the very best treatment if she became angry with the doctor? Yes, that is an *external* inhibition, inasmuch as it was a fear of the consequences that stopped her venting her anger.

Let's look back now at the example in Chapter 1 where David came round the corner and saw a teenager smashing his car window and starting to take the stereo out. David caught the teenager, and, sitting astride him on the ground, described himself as being completely overwhelmed with anger against this boy who felt he could simply go and take things that didn't belong to him. So, now he had him on the ground, at his mercy, why didn't he throttle him or smash his head up and down against the pavement? Again, the answer is 'inhibitions': but were they internal or external? Was it the fear of being hauled off to court himself on a much more serious charge than theft, or was it some deeply ingrained rule that said that you don't go smashing people's heads up and down on the pavement no matter what they've done?

Who knows? Probably a combination of the two. Either way, the episode certainly illustrates the power of such inhibitions because David clearly was, from his description, absolutely beside himself with rage.

Another example of the power of internal inhibitions – simple rules we make up for ourselves – came from a publican I was talking to recently. He described how one of his customers was arguing loudly with another and was going to hit him. The man who was about to be on the receiving end of the punch took a step back, raised his hands in a placatory gesture, and said, 'Hey, hey, hey . . . I'm over forty.' This remark, said the publican, just put a pause into the proceedings while the would-be assailant checked his memory banks to see if there really was a rule against hitting people aged over 40. Interestingly, and no doubt much to the relief of the potential recipient of the blow, by the time he had found that there wasn't really such a rule the moment had passed and he just stomped off.

Inhibitions as brakes on anger

Inhibitions, then, are in fact wonderful things – rather like the brakes on the car, they prevent us from going too far too fast. Later on in this book we are going to see how you can use inhibitions to your own benefit, so it is a good idea right now to get used to the idea that inhibitions are not just very necessary, they are extremely helpful mechanisms built right into the structure of our brains. It is also worth emphasizing that referring to 'inhibitions' in this sense is rather different from referring to somebody as 'inhibited', as a term of criticism. What we often mean in that context is that the person is constrained from displaying any emotion, not just anger, so that they may appear cold, detached, self-absorbed and unable to 'let themselves go'. But in the context of keeping our angry reactions in check, inhibitions – both internal and external – are just what we want.

Let's take one example of somebody who had not developed his inhibitions strongly enough – someone to whom, as a result, I was talking inside a prison. Brian recounted how one night he was standing at the bar, having a drink with a friend. He thinks he had probably had four or five pints of beer by the time the following incident took place. He says he was just lifting his pint mug to his mouth when somebody nearby jogged his elbow, with the result that a good amount of beer went not into his mouth but all over his face and chest. The next thing he knew, Brian had smashed his beer mug against the bar and pushed it into the man's face – thereby, of course, inflicting very severe injury indeed. The net result of those few seconds for Brian was a five-year prison sentence. It was a great pity for both men that the assailant had not worked on developing his inhibitions. Again, those inhibitions could have been external (I'll end up in prison, I'll be thrown out of the bar, the police will be called) or internal (it's not right to go around attacking people).

For most people, of course, the consequences of having undeveloped inhibitions are less dramatic than this: just a life which is impaired year after year by upsetting other people! So, there are immense benefits to be gained from learning about inhibitions and all the other techniques that we will cover later. For now it is sufficient to know about them and to know how important they are.

What holds us back?

Now we have seen how inhibitions operate, perhaps we can work out what holds people back in each of the situations we have looked at.

- Why doesn't the person who hears loud music from next door immediately go round and complain angrily? *Answer:* internal inhibition: 'It's right to be tolerant towards your neighbours'; external inhibition: 'If I do that he will probably come round here complaining as soon as I make a noise, and he will probably go around badmouthing me to all our other neighbours.'
- Why didn't Pam get angrier with her noisy-eating husband? *Answer:* internal inhibition: 'I must try and limit the amount of complaining I do, this is only a small thing'; external inhibition: 'I have probably got some bad habits too, so if I complain about his eating, he will probably start complaining about all the things I do that annoy him.'
- When people coughing during my talks used to annoy me, why did I not get angry with them and tell them to shut up or clear off? *Answer:* internal

inhibition: 'I shouldn't speak rudely to people who have come to hear me talk'; external inhibition: 'If I do that then there will be an icy-cold atmosphere for the remainder of the three days while everybody else is frightened to death of accidentally coughing.'

- Why did Nigel not snap back angrily when his wife contradicted him in public? *Answer:* internal inhibition: 'You don't wash your dirty linen in public'; external inhibition: 'People will think worse of me if I do that.'
- Why did Alan, the electrician who was asked to do too many jobs, not say 'no' to his boss straight away? *Answer:* external inhibition: his boss might think worse of him and, come the time for redundancies . . .

SUMMARY

- The ability to inhibit or control our anger is a very important ability to have. It is by no means a good idea to be 'uninhibited' where expressing our anger is concerned.
- This is not to say that you should never be angry; rather, that you will be able to control your anger. As we saw in Chapter 1, irritable and over-angry people are those whose reaction is *out of proportion to* the situation that provokes the reaction.
- Inhibitions are like the brakes of a car: sometimes they stop the car moving, but often they simply ensure the car moves at an appropriate pace.
- Inhibitions are of two main types: internal and external.

- Internal inhibitions are the thoughts and moral guidelines we have for ourselves.
- External inhibitions are the awareness of the consequences that would happen if you were to respond out of proportion to provocation.

4

Constructing a system to explain irritability and anger

The 'leaky bucket'

If we can put all that we have worked out so far into a diagram, it will help us predict when we are going to be irritable or angry and, more to the point, prevent it happening. So let's have a look at Figure 4.1, which summarizes what we have said so far about Judy's case.

Figure 4.1 Kept waiting in hospital

This is actually a particularly interesting example, because many people ask: 'What happens to the anger?' In other words, a lot of people assume that unless you 'get rid of' your anger, then it somehow just builds up inside you. This is in fact the reverse of the truth. What actually happens is that the anger just gradually dissipates. The best analogy is a leaky bucket full of water. The bucket was absolutely full in this case; Judy was very angry indeed. Nevertheless, over time, all that anger just gradually seeped away, just as water seeps out of a leaky bucket, and now in the ordinary course of things she doesn't give it a thought. (Nevertheless, if you remind her of the event, it is like pouring some more water into the bucket!)

The key concept is *doing what you think is appropriate in the situation*. In this case the mother judged that her behavior was indeed appropriate as her child might well have not received the best treatment if she had kicked up a fuss. So, even in retrospect, she still judges that she did right. By the same token, we get angry with ourselves when, in retrospect, we think we did not behave correctly. Again, the important concept is behaving in proportion to the situation, doing what you think is right in the particular situation. (Later on, we will look at why our judgement sometimes goes haywire so that on occasion we let ourselves down very badly.)

Figure 4.2 shows the same model applied to a different situation. The key difference is that here the inhibitions weren't strong enough to control the level of anger experienced by Sue. The anger therefore simply overcame her inhibitions and produced a response of 'ranting and raving'.

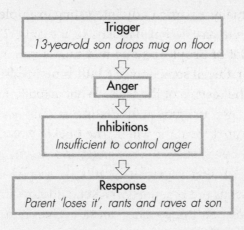

Figure 4.2 Mug breaks on floor

Actually, this does Sue a slight disservice. Certainly this is the way she described the incident – that she simply 'lost it', in other words, simply lost all control. But if that were really true, why did she not pick up the carving knife (they were in the kitchen after all) and stab her son fifty times? Clearly her inhibitions were functioning to a degree, but only at a relatively weak level; or maybe they were functioning reasonably well, but the breakage produced such an immense level of anger that they were still almost overwhelmed.

When the bucket overflows

Let's pursue this line of thought a little further by considering the case of Steve and the door left open in the pub. This fits into our model as shown in Figure 4.3.

On the face of it, this is an accurate representation of what happened. However, if you recollect the exact situation as recounted at the beginning of Chapter 1, you will see that I have omitted the fact that this was the *fifth time* the door had been left slightly ajar. On each of the previous four occasions, some extra anger had been tipped into the bucket. So, by the time person number five comes along and adds his ladleful to the bucket, the whole thing is brimful and ready to overflow – and he gives five the whole bucket full of anger. You may also recollect that Steve said when he was telling the story that the 'victim' was quite a small man. What if he had been six feet three and built to match? Possibly that would have strengthened Steve's inhibitions! Most people feel inhibited about picking a fight with someone twice their size.

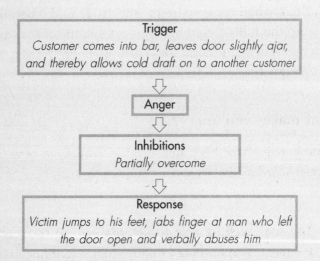

Figure 4.3 Door left open in bar

This concept of anger building up to the point where it overflows is an important one. Adrian, a senior salesman, told me the how he was repeatedly away from home on business, jetting around the world to various exotic destinations for weeks on end. While he was away his very attractive young wife Jenny took to having one affair after another. Gradually Adrian became suspicious and, after he had confronted her several times, Jenny admitted what had been going on. Though obviously hurt, Adrian thought he could cope and put it to his wife that so long as she told him everything he would be prepared to make a fresh start. So, through the course of the evening, Jenny confessed to the four affairs she had had. She went slowly and tactfully, and Adrian was able gradually to come to terms with what had happened. They went to bed, resolved that they could put it all behind them and make a fresh start.

But Jenny had remembered a fifth affair, and when they woke up the following morning, in the spirit of making a clean breast of everything, she confessed it. For Adrian, this was enough to make the bucket overflow, and they divorced.

What makes you angry?

By now you should be able to start making a tentative analysis of what makes *you* irritable and angry.

- You may well be able to identify several triggers; for most people there is more than one thing that makes them angry.

- You may even be able to quantify the amount of anger that each trigger typically produces, perhaps using a ten-point scale where 10 out of 10 is the angriest you could ever be!
- Maybe you can identify what inhibitions come into play: both your internal inhibitions (the personal morality and rules you have for your own behavior) and the external inhibitions (consequences that may befall you if you over-react).
- You may also be able to reflect upon the various responses you have made in the past when these triggers have set off your anger.

There is no need to do all that at this stage unless you want to; later on we will look at how to analyze these elements carefully, and what to do once you've analyzed them. It can be very rewarding work. But for now it may be useful to consider the kinds of questions we will be asking.

SUMMARY

- We can construct a realistic model which explains how anger and our subsequent reactions to it come about.
- It is well worth doing this because we can then analyze both our own actions and reactions, and those of others. Armed with this awareness, we can then intervene to lessen the anger we experience – and, moreover, to alter the *responses* we produce. It is those responses that people normally refer to as our 'irritability' or 'anger'.

- We will be developing this model as we go on through this book. The key headings so far are: the *trigger* (what triggers our anger); the *anger* itself (which can gradually build up, like increasing amounts of water being poured into a bucket); *inhibitions* (which stop us constantly giving vent to our anger); and the *response* (which can range from nothing at all, when we completely control our anger, through to catastrophic responses when we totally fail to control it.)
- Importantly, there is *no need* to 'let our anger out'. Very often, 'letting our anger out' simply makes it worse. Better to let it slowly seep away, like water running out from a leaky bucket.

5

Why don't other people feel angry at the things that bug me?

If we can really plot things out just as neatly and tidily as described in the previous chapter, then you would think that what triggers one person's anger would trigger the same response in another person. And, to a large extent, this is true. Most people, for example, don't like other people shouting and swearing at them. It makes them angry; it is a trigger for their anger. Most people don't like other folk stealing from them; that too is a trigger for their anger. Most people don't like sitting in interminable traffic jams. That too makes most people angry, to a greater or lesser degree.

But it is also true that people respond quite differently to some triggers. For instance, one person may get angry at the sight of teenagers playing football outside his house, whereas another may view it as part of community life.

Seeing things differently

And that is the point. It is all to do with *how we view* the event in question. If we take a hostile view of it, then it will indeed become a trigger for our anger. If we view it tolerantly and benignly, it won't.

This is not to say that we should view everything in a tolerant and benign way. As we shall see later, anger can be very useful and productive. Nevertheless, for the time being, let us just look at how things normally work.

- How come one person kept waiting in a hospital outpatient clinic became really angry whereas another person didn't? *Answer:* because the first person viewed it as inconsiderate and arrogant to schedule everybody in for a two o'clock appointment in a clinic which lasts three hours, and believes that people should show proper consideration for each other. The second person says, 'It's just one of those things,' and expects no better from people.

- Why does one man get intensely irritated by teenagers playing football outside his house, while his next-door neighbour doesn't? *Answer:* because the first person sees it not only as lacking in consideration because of the amount of noise it creates, but also as a symbol of living in a more down-market area than he would wish to. The second person sees it as part and parcel of living in a friendly, lively community.

- Why did one of the group of three men sitting by the bar door get up and confront the person who left it ajar, whereas the other two weren't bothered?

Answer: because that man believed that each person who left the door open was doing it as a deliberate provocation and felt that he was losing face in front of the other drinkers. The other two felt there was no offence meant – just that people coming into a bar are normally more concerned about getting a drink than closing the door.

- Why does one woman get angry about her husband eating in a very noisy way, while the same thing doesn't bother thousands of others at all? *Answer:* because she sees it as a symbol of the difference between their backgrounds, a constant suggestion that they really should not be married at all; for her, it epitomizes the difference between them. For others, how much noise a person makes when they eat has no significance.

- Why did I at one stage get particularly uptight about people coughing during my talks, whereas later on it didn't bother me? *Answer:* because initially I thought that they might not be paying me enough attention, or even be deliberately provoking me, whereas later I felt they were doing well to come to the course when they could be off sick.

- Why does one parent get angry when their son drops a mug on the floor and it breaks, whereas another simply says, 'Never mind', and gets him to sweep it up? *Answer:* because the first person sees it as wilful carelessness and a disregard of how much it costs to replace things, whereas the second realizes that they can easily afford to buy another mug without noticing it.

- Why does one man get angry when his partner contradicts him in public whereas another one doesn't? Because the first man views the contradiction as saying to everybody present that his wife doesn't respect him, whereas the second man views it as 'just the way she is'.

- Why does one mother get angry when she finds her daughter taking a leisurely bath whereas another doesn't? *Answer:* because the first mother said to herself that her daughter was only having a bath to avoid tidying her room, whereas the second mother was pleased to see her daughter taking good care of herself.

- Why does one father get angry with his son when he sees he has not completed his homework, whereas another father doesn't? *Answer:* Because the first father says that his son is a lazy good-for-nothing so-and-so who is trying to pull the wool over his eyes, whereas the second father says that any normal 12-year-old is bound to be more interested in watching television than doing his homework.

And so on. In other words, it is not so much the trigger *in itself* that produces the anger; it is what goes through the person's mind when prompted by the trigger.

Appraisal and judgement

Returning to our model as set out in Chapter 4, we can now extend it to apply to three of the cases we have looked at, as shown in Figures 5.1–5.3.

This one extra box we have put into our model, headed 'Appraisal/Judgement', is a very important one indeed. It means that no longer are we at the mercy of events, or 'triggers'. Now we can see that it is we ourselves who can decide what to make of these events, how to appraise or judge them. It is our appraisal or judgement which will determine whether we will get angry and to what degree. What is

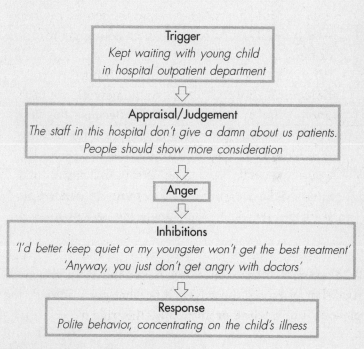

Figure 5.1 Kept waiting in hospital

more, we can actually *check out our appraisal* with that of others. For example, the man in the bar could have said to his two friends: 'Do you think these people are deliberately leaving the door open to annoy us . . . do you think everyone is laughing at us behind our backs?' Whereupon, in all probability, he would have been reassured that this was not so, that the door was just not working properly, and this might have prevented him from getting angry.

There is an important point here. Many people think that because they believe something is true, it necessarily *is* true: for instance, in this case, 'Because I believe he left the door open to annoy me, it is true that he did indeed leave the door open to annoy me.' This is very far from being the

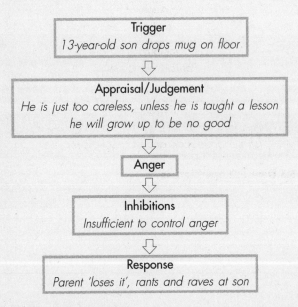

Figure 5.2 Mug breaks on floor

case; but it is an easy trap to fall into until we get used to questioning our judgements and checking them out with other people.

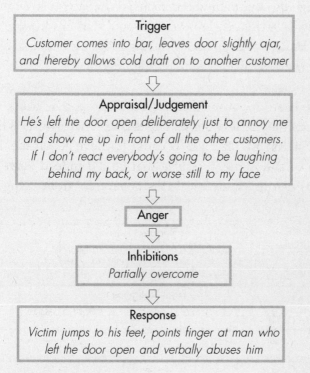

Figure 5.3 Door left open in bar

SUMMARY

- This chapter has added just one more box to our model, but it is an important box.
- That important box, 'Appraisal/Judgement', goes between 'Trigger' and 'Anger', and may totally *prevent* the trigger producing anger.
- Later, we will look at ways of examining and altering our appraisals/judgements. For the time being, it is enough to know that simply because we *think* something is true, that does not actually *make* it true.
- We are now working towards a comprehensive model with which to examine events that make us angry out of proportion to what one would reasonably expect.

6

Why isn't everybody irritated by the same things?

This sounds like pretty much the same question we asked in Chapter 5, and in a sense it is. But bear with me, because there is a significant difference. You will remember that, in Chapter 5, we asked the question: 'Why do some triggers make me angry but not other people, and vice versa?' and the answer was: because you might appraise and judge the situation one way, and other people might appraise and judge it another way. The question we are really addressing in this chapter, to put it in its fullest form, is: 'Why do I appraise and judge a situation in one way, whereas somebody else might appraise and judge it in quite a different way?'

Beliefs and judgement

So, how come you appraise and judge a situation one way while some other people appraise and judge it in another way? The answer is: 'Because of the basic beliefs we have all developed over the years.' These beliefs can be of several different kinds, for example:

- beliefs about how other people are, what the world is like, even about how we compare with other people;
- beliefs about how people are meant to behave, how people 'learn lessons', what's important in life, and so on;
- beliefs about how other people would see a particular situation, including possibly how a jury in a court of law would see it.

How do these beliefs fit in with the model we developed in the previous chapter? Clearly, our beliefs are going to influence:

- our judgement and appraisal of the trigger;
- our anger;
- our inhibitions;
- our feelings of anger;
- our response.

So now our model has another element in it, as shown in Figure 6.1.

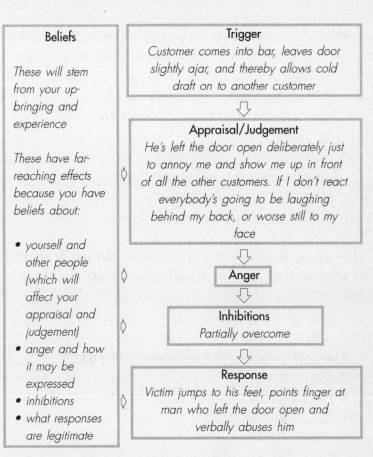

Figure 6.1 A model for analyzing irritability and anger

It's probably easiest to see how this works if we go through an example or two.

What about the man in the bar, sitting with two friends, who finally jumps up and confronts the fifth person who comes in and leaves the door open? How come it was he who jumped up, rather than one of his two friends?

Working through our model, we can see that the trigger was just the same for all three of them: so that can't be the difference.

What about the appraisal or judgement each of them makes? This will be affected by their beliefs about what other people are like. If one of them believes that people, generally, are 'all selfish bastards who don't give a damn about anyone except themselves' he will probably interpret the situation differently from someone who believes that people 'are all basically good, though sometimes their goodness needs bringing out'. So maybe that was the key difference between Steve (the one who jumped up and confronted the newcomer) and Ben and Chris (who didn't).

Now we can move on to our next box, marked 'Anger'. We can see that, primed by his beliefs about people in general, Steve's brain is already more likely to be angry than either Ben's or Chris's; and it will be 'recommending' to Steve that he makes a response in keeping with how he feels. At this stage, too, beliefs come into play. If Steve believes that 'people only learn anything if you give them a good bollocking' then the chances are that his brain will be recommending something different from those of Ben and Chris, who believe for the most part that 'the only way people learn anything is when they are allowed to sit down and think things through'.

From here we move on to 'Inhibitions'. By now we can see that Steve, who thinks that people are 'all selfish bastards who don't give a damn about anyone except themselves' and that 'people only learn anything if you give them a good bollocking', is already thinking in terms of a pretty hostile response. But possibly his inhibitions will tone it down. If he believes that 'you don't show your anger in public', that might keep him under control. Equally, if he believes that 'if you confront somebody they are liable to attack you' then that too will restrain him, so long as the person leaving the door open is bigger than he is. On the other hand, if he believes that 'if somebody deliberately provokes you then you've got to show them who's boss,' this is unlikely to do much to keep his anger in check.

Finally, then, we come to his response. We can see that beliefs are going to play a part here. If he believes that 'It's all right thumping somebody but you don't ever use a weapon,' his response is clearly going to be of a different order than if he believes that 'If you're going to pick a fight with somebody you have to be tooled up.'

So we can see in this example that the beliefs Steve holds are going to affect him at every stage. And these beliefs are *nothing to do with the situation in question*; they are beliefs he holds day in, day out. So if Steve wanted to radically alter the way he is, the way he feels and the way he reacts, he could work on his beliefs, perhaps bring them a bit closer to those of Ben and Chris. We'll see how later on.

What about Anne and her 12-year-old in the bath? Anne, you'll remember, got really angry with her daughter because she wasn't tidying her room. Anne's next-door neighbour, Elaine, also has fairly young children and she has always reacted differently to them in the face of stress. So let's have a look at how our model would compare Anne and Elaine.

Again, the trigger or situation would have to be just the same: how would Elaine react if her 12-year-old had been resolutely not tidying her room, and how would this compare with Anne's reaction?

Let's have a look at the judgement or appraisal that each would make in the face of this event. Anne's judgement is influenced by the fact that she believes that her daughter 'deliberately does everything she can to annoy me'. Elaine, on the other hand, believes that 'Children don't annoy you deliberately, but they are naturally selfish and only lose that as they get older'. Anne, therefore, is inclined to see her 12-year-old's behavior as deliberate defiance, designed to provoke her; Elaine, on the other hand, views her daughter's similar behavior as a piece of thoughtlessness typical of a child of that age. As a result, Anne is inclined to be angry, Elaine much less so.

As a result of this belief, Anne's angry brain is already recommending some kind of angry response. Unfortunately, Anne also believes that 'You get nowhere by coddling kids,' with the corresponding implication that 'a firm hand', either metaphorically or literally, is what is required. Elaine thinks differently. Even when she does get angry (which, you will be pleased to hear, she does sometimes) her basic belief is that 'Children need a good example set for them.' So, while she doesn't mind confronting issues with her children, and them knowing that she is angry and hearing it in her voice, she does try hard not to 'shout and scream at them', and certainly doesn't believe in smacking them.

What about inhibitions? Anne believes that if her neighbours hear her 'going over the top' in terms of shouting or smacking her youngster they will report her to social services. She says this is one of the main things that makes her able sometimes to control her temper. Elaine believes that it is simply not right to shout and scream at young children, and certainly not to hit them.

In terms of response, Anne thinks that 'A good smack never did anyone any harm,' while Elaine believes that 'Adults hitting children is simply bullying.'

Beliefs and behavior

One of the interesting points raised by the example of Anne and Elaine is that it doesn't matter whether beliefs are right or not, they still influence the behavior of the person who holds them. For instance, Anne may be correct in believing that 'Kids do all they can to deliberately annoy you' and Elaine may be wrong in believing that 'Children are just selfish by nature and grow out of it eventually.' It really doesn't matter who is right and who is wrong: both are heavily influenced by their own beliefs. You sometimes even see the paradoxical situation where Elaine's child may be annoying her quite deliberately but, because Elaine believes what she does, she not only leads a calmer life but also sets a better example for her child.

Let's look at another example, this time involving flirting. Fiona and Graham live on a new housing development, and Graham has quite serious problems with jealousy. Hannah and Ian are another young couple who live nearby. Fiona and Hannah are good friends and are very similar in many respects. Unlike Graham, however, Ian has no problems with jealousy.

On several occasions Graham and Ian have faced more or less the same 'trigger'. From time to time both couples find themselves at the same party – in fact, very often they will actually all go to the party together. Both Fiona and Hannah are warm, friendly and extrovert young women who like to have an uninhibited time simply in terms of dancing, drinking and feeling the pleasure of having friends around them. Graham and Ian appraise these 'triggers' in quite different ways. Graham believes that if a woman is married then she shouldn't be showing any interest in any other man, and this is what he perceives Fiona as doing. Ian, on the other hand, believes that it is only natural for women to show an interest in men and vice versa. He simply believes that if you are married then 'You shouldn't take it any further than the interest stage.' So, as a result of the same events, Graham becomes angry whereas Ian doesn't. Graham's angry brain is recommending to him an angry response, whereas Ian's is not.

In terms of inhibitions, Graham believes that it is wrong to hit anybody, and certainly somebody you love, so even though angry he will not respond that way. (Interestingly, Ian is not totally averse to getting into fights; he does not believe that is totally wrong. Fortunately, however, he rarely becomes angry.) Graham also believes that if he 'addresses the issue head on' then (a) Fiona will think he is a 'wimp' for being jealous, and (b) this will put a damper on the fun they might have at any future party.

In terms of responses, Graham believes it is wrong to hit people so that is ruled out. He also believes it is undesirable to shout or to address the issue head on, so he tends not to do this. His beliefs about sulking, however, are not quite so negative; so that is what he tends to end up doing. Ian, on the other hand, believes that 'Sulking is something women do,' so even when angry doesn't tend to respond like that.

It is clear from these examples that our beliefs can have an all-pervasive effect on us – not just on irritability and anger but on every aspect of our feelings and emotions: jealousy, anxiety, depression, anything you care to mention.

Beliefs and other people

Once a year my mother and I go off on two or three days' holiday, just the two of us (my family stays behind and has a bit of respite). A couple of years ago we found ourselves in Paris, in an extremely nice hotel which we could certainly never have afforded had it not been for a very special offer at the local travel agent. Anyway, once there, we look around for what to do. Tickets available from the hotel include an evening at the Moulin Rouge which is, as you know, a kind of review bar for tourists. It looks good, and of all the attractions on offer it is the only one we have heard of. The only snag is that it is expensive: 900 francs per person for the evening – that's about £80 or $125. However, this (it seems) includes everything: dinner, drinks, review, the lot. So we sign up, and the next evening off we go. The Moulin Rouge consists of a big stage on which a lot of girls strut their stuff – and an even bigger area where about five million tourists eat their dinners at tables crammed more closely together than you have ever seen before. We are given a terrific table, right next to the stage, are given complimentary drinks shortly followed by the first course of our dinner, and sit back for a good evening. As the show starts, I notice a very small card sitting on the table, pick it up and just manage to read what it says in the gloom. My hazy brain does a slow translation: 'minimum drinks order 600 francs per person'. I am stunned. Not only having paid handsomely for our two tickets, we are now faced with having to pay another substantial sum for drinks. I am not even sure I have got that much money on me. Everywhere I look I see twenty-stone bouncers, and begin to realize the true meaning of the phrase 'tourist trap'.

My mother is pretty engrossed in the show. I am feeling sort of nauseous, and, even from the inside, can tell I must look glazed. The Third Act finishes and there is a gap before the band starts up to herald the Fourth Act. At this point I mention, calmly of course, that there is a card on the table that says there is a minimum drinks order of £50 or $85 per person.

And this is where beliefs come in. Me, I believe that all big cities are the same and that if you go to a tourist trap then you expect to get trapped. My mother, she has had good holidays in France so, quick as a flash, she says: 'No, it's all right, the French are nice' – without taking her eyes off the stage. It is a simple belief, deeply embedded and has ramifications for a thousand and one situations that might arise in France. (And, thank goodness, she was right: the card's strictures didn't apply to us.)

Not long after the Moulin Rouge experience, I came across another example of an extended version of 'French people are nice.' I was walking along a promenade in a quiet coastal resort, and coming towards me was a man of about 25 who clearly had significant learning difficulties. He had a rucksack which was causing him some trouble: he had managed to get it properly hooked over one shoulder, but the other side was sort of pinning his arm halfway behind him. This posture will be familiar to anyone who has ever tried to put a rucksack on; and it's much more easily sorted out by someone else than by the wearer. So this man simply walked up and stood in front of me without saying a word; and I sorted out his rucksack.

What does that say about this man's beliefs about other people? *'Other people are nice.'* So nice, in fact, that if you are having trouble with your rucksack, all you have to do is go and stand in front of a random person and he or she will sort you out. You don't even have to say anything!

So, not only do underlying beliefs influence just about every moment of your life; but doing a bit of work on your beliefs can pay off handsomely. We'll look at how to do this later on in the book.

Where do beliefs come from?

Some of you reading this might be wondering where our beliefs come from. Well, clearly they come from our experiences. Many of them come from early experience (our childhood, school and upbringing) and are never revised. Sometimes, for example, people are taught as children that everybody in the world is out for what they can get, so you have to watch your back. Others, although they are not explicitly taught such lessons, pick them up for themselves through observing others. Equally, many people are taught as children that 'people are basically good', or have had the sort of upbringing which has led them to believe that this is the case, whether or not it was spelt out for them.

On the basis of these 'mega-beliefs' we make rules for ourselves. For instance, if I believe that everyone is out for what they can get, I will have a series of sub-beliefs along the lines of 'I must keep my wits about me,' 'You have to watch everybody like a hawk or they'll take advantage of you,' and 'If you give someone an inch they'll take a mile.' Equally, if I believe that people are basically good I will have a series of sub-beliefs along the lines of 'We must trust each other in order to flourish,' 'The best place to relax is in the company of others,' and so on.

SUMMARY

- We set out in this chapter to answer the question of why a particular situation would irritate one person and not another.
- We came to the conclusion that it is to do with our beliefs about ourselves, other people, the nature of the world, how people are meant to behave and how we are meant to behave.
- These beliefs are developed over the years through our experiences and observations, often based on the things we are told when we are young.
- We found that our beliefs also underlie our inhibitions. Some people believe that you shouldn't ever hit anybody, even if it's called 'smacking'. Other people believe you mustn't hit anybody unless it's someone much smaller than yourself, like your child. Other people believe that it's wrong to shout. Other people

believe that it's right to talk things through with people even if they are very young. Other people believe that to set a good example is very important. All these beliefs will form part of our internal inhibitions. Others are much more constrained by the likely results of their actions, so believe that it is ill-advised to pick a fight with somebody bigger than you, as you're likely to get hurt; these beliefs form part of their external inhibitions.

- People even have beliefs about the kind of responses it's okay to make. Some people believe that an obviously aggressive response is inappropriate, but sulking would be okay; and so on.
- All this knowledge about beliefs and their influence forms another important area that we will be able to use to our benefit when we come to Part Two of this book.

7

Why am I sometimes more irritable than at other times?

Up to now we've concentrated largely on the question, 'Why do some people get angry more easily than other people?' And we've come up with lots of answers – or at least, we could work out lots of answers for lots of different situations if we wanted to by going through our model. Some of the answers might be as follows:

- John gets more angry than Ken because John finds himself in more anger-making situations than Ken does.
- Laura gets more angry than Mona because Laura tends to judge and appraise situations differently from the way Mona does.
- Norma gets more angry than Olive because her inhibitions aren't so well developed.
- Pete seems to get more angry than Quentin because Pete will countenance more hostile responses than Quentin does. For example, Pete will shout and threaten while Quentin tends to sulk.

- Rachel gets more angry than Sarah because Rachel believes that other people are basically a self-centred lot who can't be trusted, so she tends to misinterpret some situations.

And so on.

So, we can now make some more informed and reliable judgements about why some people get more angry than others, or seem to be more angry than others (because of the way they respond when they are angry). And this is good, because if we want to be one of those people who is angry less often we can already see that there are going to be some very powerful things we can achieve. We have a nice model which we can apply systematically in your own particular case.

Moods

But for many people it is the *variation* in their irritability that really concerns them: in other words, some days they feel really irritable, other days they don't. If you are one of these people then you will know that this variation causes major problems for people around you, because they never know 'what mood you're going to be in'. So they can never relax properly with you, and that in turn means that the feelings of intimacy and closeness that would otherwise develop between you and them simply don't have a chance to take root.

Moreover, you will also know that this causes major problems for yourself – not just in how it impairs the intimacy of relationships, but also because you continually feel as though you have 'let yourself down'. If you have these big variations in irritability you will sometimes look back on things you did yesterday, or even earlier on today, and feel embarrassed or ashamed by them. For, although they seemed perfectly sensible and justifiable at the time, now you can see that you were being excessively irritable – you were in 'a bad mood'. (Actually, they don't always seem that sensible at the time; maybe you know when you're feeling irritable, and that's a very bad feeling. The trouble is that it seems very difficult to 'snap out of it' at the time, and indeed it is.)

The good news is that there are all sorts of things that we can do to keep ourselves in a 'stable mood'. But first we need to focus on the key concept of 'mood'.

In terms of our model, like 'Beliefs', it influences all four of the major boxes from 'Appraisal/Judgement' downwards, so that the model now looks like Figure 7.1.

How does this work? First of all, take the way mood influences the way we appraise and judge things. Try thinking of Tim, who does indeed have problems with his moods and who will see things quite differently depending on whether he's in a good mood or a bad mood. He drew up a table to show just how differently things could look to him (Table 7.1).

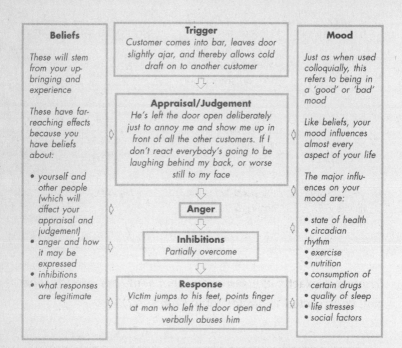

Figure 7.1 A model for analyzing irritability and anger

TABLE 7.1: GOOD MOODS AND BAD MOODS, 1

Situation	How Tim sees things when he's in a good mood	How Tim sees things when he's in a bad mood
Neighbours playing music next door	Cheerful and symbolizing the cheerfulness of life	Selfish and inconsiderate
Neighbours' children playing football in the street	Communal thing to do; sometimes Tim would even join in	Selfish and inconsiderate; Tim will watch for the ball going on his garden

People coming into the pub when Tim is sitting near the door	'The pub filling up nicely' – regardless of whether they shut the door or leave it open	Thoughtless and a nuisance
Tim's wife contradicts him in public	'A chance for a good bit of banter'	'Totally out of order'
Sees his wife flirting with other men	'All good fun – there's nothing in it'	'Totally out of order'

Uma has exactly the same problem with her moods, and she constructed a similar table (Table 7.2).

TABLE 7.2: GOOD MOODS AND BAD MOODS, 2		
Situation	How Uma sees things when she's in a good mood	How Uma sees things when she's in a bad mood
Her husband eating noisily	Doesn't notice	'Totally unbearable'
Her children dropping and breaking things	'Accidents will happen – I've broken enough things myself in my time'	'Drives me completely mad – it's just pure carelessness'
Waiting for two hours in an outpatient clinic with her child	Likely to see it as a chance to get to know the other mums	Storms straight into the clinic room and has it out with the doctor there and then

| Her husband 'telling all and sundry what they've been talking about' | Never takes a positive view of her husband talking about things she had regarded as 'between them'; however, 'best just to leave it' | 'The last straw – I just feel like walking out on him at that very moment' |
| Children are disobedient | 'It's no use getting het up about what your kids do, there's no changing them' | 'I wonder why I ever had them' |

It's clear from these few examples that anybody who is in a remotely similar situation to either Tim or Uma will be having a great deal of trouble making sense of their life. One day they're up, the next day they're down. One day they're laughing and joking with people; another day they're snapping their heads off. Worse than that, it can vary from one half-hour to another. So what kind of things do we have to watch out for to keep our mood steady? Some of the main factors are:

- Illness: mental illnesses (such as depression) or physical illnesses (such as viral infections) can both disrupt your mood.
- Routine: it is very important to maintain a fairly consistent routine in terms of times of eating and sleeping, to maintain a steady 'circadian rhythm'.

Otherwise you find yourself in a permanent state of 'jetlag', which is very disruptive.

• Exercise: humans are built for activity, and during phases when we don't get this we are liable to be that much more irritable.

• Diet: some people eat lots of sugar-rich food which sends their blood sugar level sky-high and then correspondingly low. Other people feed themselves so poorly that they are effectively suffering from malnutrition.

• Drugs: routinely consumed drugs such as caffeine, alcohol and nicotine are vastly underestimated in their effect. Recreational drugs can also devastate one's mood.

• Sleep: getting insufficient sleep on a regular basis is bad news indeed.

• Stress: having too much to do, too many pressures on you, tasks you find difficult to achieve, and other life stresses take a severe toll on your moods.

• Social factors: arguments with friends, relatives and workmates; bereavement, separation and divorce; simply feeling lonely – these are just some of the social factors that can affect our mood.

If you know that you sometimes get irritable, the chances are that there are several items on that list which look familiar to you. The good news is that we can work on them, and later on in Part Two of this book, we will see exactly what to do.

There are tremendous pay-offs here. Most people much prefer someone who is 'the same every day' to someone who is 'downright moody'.

Case study: Georgina

Georgina went through a period of three years in her late teens when, she said, she would 'snap anybody's head off who looked at me in the wrong way'. It turns out this wasn't quite true; there were just some days when she acted this way. Other days she was a thoroughly agreeable young person with lots of friends, a nice family life and occasional boyfriends. It turned out that the reason she was sometimes so irritable is that she was prone to get quite depressed, mainly on account of her boyfriends being only 'occasional'. When she did feel depressed, however, she was snappy in the extreme, and even people's attempts to cheer her up provoked an abrasive reaction. Unsurprisingly, some of her friends drifted away, while even the ones that remained tended to treat her with some caution.

The solution to Georgina's problems was twofold.

- First, she gradually worked on her depression until she settled in a fairly consistently happy mood. This was difficult, because she had set up a vicious circle whereby her depression caused her irritability, which caused some of her friends to desert her, which in turn exacerbated her depression. Nevertheless, she implemented three significant measures which helped her to be happier.

- Second, and while she was working on her depression, she also worked on the 'Response' box in our model. In other words, she trained herself to 'button my lip and count to ten' whenever she felt like snapping.

The net result is that both she and her friends feel that life is now more predictable and, partly as a result, more rewarding.

SUMMARY

- Sometimes you may be more irritable than at other times. One day you may be in a good mood, the next in a bad mood. The key concept here is 'mood'.
- There are lots of factors that influence our mood, notably illness, routine, exercise, diet, drugs, sleep patterns, life stresses and social factors.
- We can work on these (as we shall see in Part Two) so that, if we want, we can be not only difficult to anger, but reliable and consistent: 'the same every day'!

8

Is it always wrong to be angry?

Briefly, the answer is 'no'. However, perhaps it is always wrong to be irritable.

Why is it not wrong to be angry? Simply because the question of whether anger is 'wrong' or not doesn't really arise. Rather like gravity, anger is part of life; so to start questioning whether it is good or bad is to head up something of a blind alley.

This is not the whole story, however. Perhaps we can give a better answer by asking what purpose anger serves. Most of the things that are 'part of the human condition' do serve a purpose and one suspects that anger is no exception.

Anger and disapproval

One purpose is to help to produce 'socialization' in other people: in other words, to encourage other people to behave in the way we would like them to – or, more accurately, to discourage other people from behaving in a way we don't want them to. The distinction is not just a question of semantics. It *is*, in fact, possible to influence a person's behavior much more by encouragement than by discouragement. This point was encapsulated by the old cartoon depicting a fearsomely old-fashioned school with a notice on the wall reading 'the beatings will continue until morale improves', neatly making the point that some things simply cannot be produced by beatings – or anger, or any other negative means. Nevertheless, for our present purposes it is worth noting that anger does indeed serve a function of discouraging behavior that we don't want.

The trouble with this is that if we happen to be rather intolerant individuals, then we can feel there is a tremendous lot of 'behavior we don't want', which in turn means that we will spend an awful lot of our lives being angry. (In this context the concept of 'zero tolerance' seems to me a disastrous one. For the state to discuss, advocate and encourage a principle of 'zero tolerance' seems doomed to produce adverse consequences across the board.

On the other hand, if we ourselves are fairly tolerant individuals, and know what behavior we like and dislike in each other, then anger can be a highly appropriate response, though of course in moderation. Maybe 'anger' is not really the right word in this context; possibly 'annoyance' is nearer the mark. If somebody cares for us and cares about what we think, then to see that their behavior has annoyed us even slightly would be sufficient to influence them.

One piece of good news is that there is much less undesirable behavior than we think. Take the case of Walter and Yvonne, who were out for a day trip to the seaside with their children aged ten and twelve. It was 12.30 p.m., just coming up to lunchtime, when the family was walking past an ice-cream van near the beach. The ten-year-old asked for an ice cream, to which his father replied: 'No, it'll be lunchtime in a quarter of an hour.' The boy was not to be pacified, however, and persisted in trying to persuade and cajole his father to buy an ice cream, refusing even to move on past the van.

His father's response was to insist: 'If I say no, I mean no. If you really want one, then you can have one after lunch.'

This was no good; the ten-year-old wanted his ice cream there and then, and achieving this was evidently becoming more important than life itself. His father, for his part, felt that it was important to make a stand and show his son that you can't always have what you want.

Well, I will spare you the ghastly details, but suffice to say that that was the end of their day trip as any sort of enjoyable enterprise.

I talked to Walter about this afterwards in terms of the personality characteristics being displayed by the ten-year-old boy. What it boiled down to was that he was being very assertive and very persevering, both of which characteristics his father thought were admirable ones he'd want in his son when he became an adult. So, paradoxically, he felt he should be encouraging such characteristics rather than just getting angry when they are displayed!

This is only one small example of how tricky it can be to judge and appraise situations. Much more often than it seems at first sight, the characteristics that are being displayed when we are tempted to get annoyed are ones which, in other circumstances, we would actually value rather than condemn.

What it boils down to is that anger – or at least annoyance – can be entirely appropriate to express disapproval of other people's behavior, *when we really are sure that we disapprove of it.*

Anger and motivation

Anger/annoyance also has another purpose, namely to provide us with the motivation to do things we otherwise wouldn't do.

One of the angriest times I have ever experienced was when our nine-month-old daughter got locked in the car on a very hot summer's day, with the keys also in the car. Nearby was a man from the emergency rescue service who wouldn't help us in spite of our being members.

It was the middle of June, Amelia was in her buggy on the back seat of the car, and my wife had inadvertently locked the keys in the car. Distraught, she left Amelia and the car and went out on to the street, with our other daughter who was two, to seek help. As if the gods were really with her, she spotted a man wearing the uniform of the rescue service just fifty yards down the street. She explained her plight, to which the man replied 'Are you a member?'

Patricia said yes, she was, to which the reply was: 'Have you got your membership card?'

Patricia said: 'Yes, it's in the car.'

And the man's response was: 'Well, I can't do anything without your membership card.'

However, in a fit of generosity he loaned her a coin to phone me up so that I could come with the spare keys. I got there as quickly as I could, gave Patricia the spare keys and went to speak to the 'rescue' man.

I say 'speak to', but that is perhaps misrepresenting what followed. I gave him a full and thorough account of what I thought of him and his family, lasting a good five minutes and much to the entertainment of passers-by.

Now, if you had asked me one sunny June afternoon to go and advise a representative of a road rescue service on how he should behave if somebody has locked themselves out of – and their baby into – a car, I would probably have said that I had better things to do. It was only the absolute rage I felt that fired me up to enthusiastically advise this particular man.

The same thing applies when we hear stories of people going to help strangers beaten up in the street, or countries declaring war on other countries that are trampling over the human rights of their neighbours.

How much anger is enough?

So, the interesting question arises as to how much anger we need to display in order to influence other people's behavior. Clearly, there is a vast range available. As we said earlier, if a person cares about you and what you think, then your expression of the slightest hint of annoyance will probably be sufficient.

In fact, different rules hold good for physically violent situations such as war. So, for the moment, let us confine ourselves to non-violent interpersonal situations.

With anger, as with most other things, it is not a question of 'the more the better' if you want to be effective. The inverted U-curve, sometimes known as Aristotle's golden mean, holds good here. If you like graphs, this is the thing for you. It is normally drawn as shown in Figure 8.1. It suggests that a little bit of anger will have some effect; a bit more anger will have more effect; but if you increase the anger too much, then the effect comes down again.

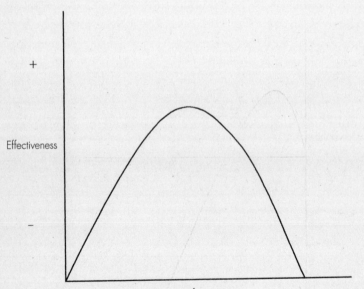

Figure 8.1 The traditional inverted U-curve

Actually, this 'traditional' inverted U is not quite what is needed in the case of anger. More accurate is the version shown in Figure 8.2. What this shows is that the 'best' amount of anger is just a small amount. If you increase it, the effectiveness decreases. And if you increase it even more, then the effectiveness is negative; in other words, what you are doing is counter-productive, and, far from influencing your target in the required direction, will provoke them to 'dig their heels in' or 'react against you', or however you like to describe it.

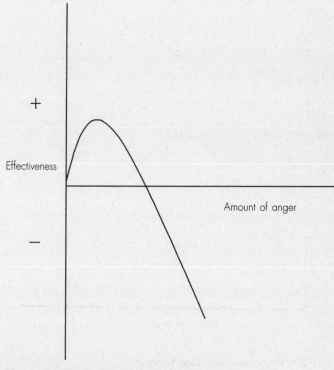

Figure 8.2 Graph showing effective anger

If you don't like graphs, forget this and think about someone who's not very good at making a cup of coffee. For the sake of argument, let's agree that the best amount of coffee to put in a mug is one rounded teaspoonful. So Andy comes along, puts two rounded teaspoonfuls in his mug, adds boiling water and milk, sits down to enjoy it and finds it doesn't taste very nice. Of course, he doesn't know *why* it doesn't taste very nice because he's no good at making coffee. So what does he do? He goes and puts in a third teaspoonful, which, of course, makes it taste even worse. And if he's really hopeless, he may even go back and add a fourth.

Now, the coffee example seems ridiculous to most of us because we know how much coffee to put in a mug. Not to Andy, though, because he's never made his own coffee before, and he has no idea how to do it. This is an exact parallel with some people and their anger. They start off by displaying much too much anger and find that they don't get the desired result. So what do they do then? Get even angrier still. To an onlooker this is as bizarre as Andy putting even more coffee in his mug when he already has too much. To the person concerned, however, it doesn't seem like that. 'If that much anger didn't work, then perhaps twice as much will,' they seem to be saying.

In summary, anger, like pepper, is best in very small amounts, if at all.

Does irritability have a purpose?

What about irritability? Does the same argument hold good there? The answer seems to be 'no', because the essence of irritability is that it is unjustified and inappropriate – more a reflection of your mood than of anything anybody else has done.

I have heard it said that the advantage of being known as 'irritable' is that it keeps everybody else 'on their toes'. The implication is that you will always be treated as carefully as though you were at your most irritable, because even when you are in a good mood people put it down to the fact that they are 'handling you with kid gloves'. So they carry on treating you that way.

For most people this has only a superficial attraction. Most people want to be respected and liked at work and in social situations, and liked and loved at home. While irritability may force others to *cover up* the manifestations of their disrespect and dislike for you, it does no more than that. There seems no shortcut to acquiring respect, liking and love, short of earning it. Being irritable normally means starting off with an overdraft.

SUMMARY

- Anger is okay in the sense that most people get angry at some times; it's something we have to live with.
- Nevertheless, it does seem that we can influence the behavior of those around us much more by positive means than becoming angry.

- Even so, anger – or at least annoyance – is a reasonable way of expressing displeasure at what somebody else does.
- In terms of *how much* anger is appropriate, it is almost always *a lot less then we think*. Indeed, too much anger is not only ineffective, it is distinctly counter-productive.
- Irritability is never justified. After all, it is *defined* as 'unjustified anger or irritation'!

PART TWO

Sorting It Out

Part Two of this book is all about solutions.

Having read Part One, you now know a lot about irritability and anger. However, knowing about a problem is not the same as solving that problem. So in this part of the book we examine all the possible solutions.

There are several ways of reading this part. Each chapter title gives you a pretty good idea of what is in the chapter and why you might want to read it. So you can, if you want, go straight to the chapters you think are most relevant to you and read those first. In fact, you will find it works even if you *just* read those, and omit the others. You can 'pick and choose'.

Alternatively, you can read steadily from here to the end, including every chapter whether or not it seems relevant at first sight. This isn't a bad idea, because some of the content may turn out to apply to you even though it might not have looked like it on first consideration. I have tried to include lots of examples (there are twenty-four, in fact), and some of them come up repeatedly; you might well find that you can easily identify with some of these cases.

At the end of each chapter is a summary and a project (or more than one!) to do. It is those projects which are really going to make a good impact for you if you follow them through.

Whichever way you tackle this part of the book, I hope you find it useful.

9

Getting a handle on the problem: The trigger

If you think back to Chapter 4, where we were starting to work on the model of irritability and anger, you may remember that the most basic model looked like Figure 9.1. This diagram doesn't contain all sorts of boxes that we added as the model developed, but does contain three of the most essential ones. We can see that if any one of these three boxes is altered, then the whole sequence of irritability and anger comes to an end.

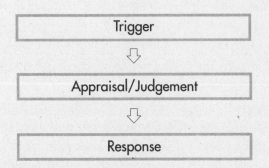

Figure 9.1 A model for analyzing irritability and anger

For example, take Gerry, whose trigger is his neighbours playing music too loud. If that trigger doesn't happen, then the irritability and anger don't happen. Equally, even if the trigger does happen (the neighbours play their music), he still won't respond with anger if he appraises it as 'just them having a bit of fun – the thing to do is live and let live.' And finally, even if the trigger does happen and he appraises it as 'those awful people again – they need a good sorting out,' he will still not display any irritability and anger if he takes himself off to see his friend in the adjoining road or puts his own earphones on.

So, this simple model yields three possible solutions:

1 somehow or other have the neighbours not play their music;
2 appraise it in a different light; or
3 respond in some different way.

In this particular example, which would you say is the best solution? Personally I'd go for either number 1 (ideally) or number 2.

Or what about Anne, who said she completely 'lost it' when she found her twelve-year-old daughter washing her hair in the bath instead of tidying her room? Again, there are three possible options:

1 she could have somehow got her daughter to tidy her room (we'll go into how later on);
2 she could have appraised it a different way ('Well, at least she's keeping herself clean'); or

3 she could have responded in a different way, for
   example by taking herself off, calming down, and
   telling her daughter (again) that she expected her
   room to be tidied after she'd finished her bath.

Again it's a matter of personal opinion, but possibly numbers
(2) or (3) would be the front-runners in this case.

And what about Steve, who gave a good roasting to the
fifth guy who left the bar door open? In that case he could
have

1 removed the trigger (by moving to a different table
   after the first couple of times);
2 appraised it differently ('There are worse things in
   life than having to push a door closed every twenty
   minutes'); or
3 responded differently, perhaps by asking each
   person to shut the door.

Possibly either (1) or (3) might be better in this case.

So, even with a simple three-box analysis some reasonably good solutions present themselves.

The odd thing is that in each of these cases the individual concerned had taken on a sort of 'victim role', as
though they could do nothing about what was happening.
So Gerry blamed the neighbours ('What can you do if you've
got neighbours like that?'), Anne told the story as just one
more example of how 'difficult' her daughter was, and Steve
saw his experience in the bar as one more example of how
'ignorant' other people are.

Keeping a diary

In fact, there's no need to be a victim: there are lots of things we can do once we have 'got a handle on' the problem. In other words, *once you know, reliably, what triggers your anger or irritability you are halfway to sorting it out.* And really to get to know what triggers it, you have to keep a diary.

The best form of diary to keep, in the first instance, is illustrated by Diary 1. You will see there are just two boxes: one for you to write about the trigger, and the other one for you to write about how you responded. There is one blank copy of this diary included here, and there are ten more in the Appendix (pp. 278–85).

These diaries are very important indeed. Their function is, as I've just said, to enable you to get a handle on what makes you irritable and angry. If you can do this, you are halfway home. So exactly how do you fill them in? The answer is: it is best to fill in a diary sheet each time you get irritable or angry, and to do it *as soon as possible* after the incident. It is also a good idea to make your accounts as complete as possible. On the following pages I have reproduced more or less what was filled in by several people we have already described, when they kept their diaries.

Diary 1

Keep a record of when you get irritable or angry. Fill it in as soon as possible after the event. Note as clearly as possible what triggered your irritability/anger, and how you responded

TRIGGER (INCLUDE DAY, DATE AND TIME)

RESPONSE (WHAT DID YOU DO?)

Example (a)

TRIGGER (INCLUDE DAY, DATE AND TIME)

Saturday 3 June, 11.15 a.m. The kids next door were playing football in the street outside. They had already been across the lawn several times and finally the football hit our front window.

RESPONSE (WHAT DID YOU DO?)

I went straight out, took the ball off the kids, rang the bell next door and gave their mother a piece of my mind.

Example (b)

TRIGGER (INCLUDE DAY, DATE AND TIME)

Friday 28 February, 9.30 p.m. Several people had already come into the bar and left the door open. We were sitting just by the door, three of us, and it was very cold outside, so there was a draft when the door was left open. None of them gave a damn about us, just marched straight in and went up and got their drinks. It wasn't until about half a dozen people had done this that I reacted.

RESPONSE (WHAT DID YOU DO?)

To the first few people that came in I didn't do anything. But when the fifth guy came in I just got up and threatened him. I stood in front of him and told him exactly what I thought of him and his type so that the whole bar could hear. That was pretty much an end to the evening. The other two didn't really get settled again and we went home after about half an hour.

Example (c)

TRIGGER (INCLUDE DAY, DATE AND TIME)

Tuesday 3 June, 8.00 p.m. We were sitting, eating a meal when, yet again, my husband was chewing his food so loudly that half the street would be able to hear him. I'm sure he does it just to annoy me, or at least he doesn't care that it does annoy me. What he does is to get his mouth full of food and then spend ages chewing every mouthful and talking to me while he does it.

RESPONSE (WHAT DID YOU DO?)

I didn't say or do anything, I just felt really tight inside. And I didn't talk to him properly and I just felt sad being married to him. I've told him about it dozens of times before, so what's the point going on about it again? But somehow it just symbolizes the way he is – he doesn't care about me, just about him.

Example (d)

TRIGGER (INCLUDE DAY, DATE AND TIME)

Wednesday 17 September, 5.30 p.m. Ian, who is 13, dropped a coffee mug on the kitchen floor and it shattered. There was no coffee in it, just the mug – but that's typical of him. He just doesn't care, he thinks money grows on trees and anything he breaks I will replace.

RESPONSE (WHAT DID YOU DO?)

I completely lost it. I shouted at him and told him to get out of my sight. It took me a good half hour to one hour to calm down at all. Even when he was upstairs I went up and told him again.

Example (e)

TRIGGER (INCLUDE DAY, DATE AND TIME)

Wednesday 7 June, 3.30 p.m. The boss asked me to go out to Scudamore Avenue to sort out a call there. The occupier wanted some wiring looked at that they weren't sure was safe. The thing is that the boss knew I already had plenty of work on and he was just taking advantage of me because he knew I wouldn't complain.

RESPONSE (WHAT DID YOU DO?)

I was just very short with him so that he would know I was irritated and thought he was out of order. But I finished off the work that had to be done in the base and then went off and sorted this other person's wiring out. And I did the jobs properly.

Example (f)

TRIGGER (INCLUDE DAY, DATE AND TIME)

Thursday 10 April, 6.30 p.m. I had been on at my daughter all day long to tidy her room and she kept saying she would do it in a minute, or a bit later. Then at about half-past six I found her sitting in the bath just washing her hair – and deliberately provoking me, saying, 'What are you going to do about that then?'

RESPONSE (WHAT DID YOU DO?)

I really let rip. I shouted and screamed at her for – it must have been ten minutes. She went really pale, and looking back at it I was over the top. But it worked, she did tidy her room later on.

Example (g)

TRIGGER (INCLUDE DAY, DATE AND TIME)

Wednesday 27 July, 4.15 p.m. There was no real trigger beyond the fact that I was feeling very stressed out, as usual. At work these days there are just so many demands on me from so many different people that I cannot possibly fulfil everything that everybody expects of me. Therefore, when Phil just made some throwaway remark, that was the last straw.

I just blew my top at Phil and criticized him for his attitude. It was totally unfair, what he had said was just by way of banter. Me blowing my top was much more to do with my state of mind than Phil's attitude. But anyway I apologized to him later on and things seem to be okay now, more or less.

Reading your diary

Well, never mind reading your diary for the moment. Let's first of all get good at reading other people's diaries.

Even before that, let's recap on what the point of reading these diaries is: it is *to obtain insight into what makes you irritable and angry, so that you can take action about it.* And, to do that, you will first of all have to develop the skill of reading diaries astutely.

Now let's take the examples in order.

First of all, look again at example (a), in which Colin tells how he was driven to distraction by his neighbour's kids playing football in the street. Which of the following possibilities do you think was the trigger:

1 the kids repeatedly running across his grass;
2 the football hitting his window;
3 the thought that his neighbours showed no consideration for him;
4 the belief that kids playing in the street makes the area look poor?

In this particular case the answer Colin gave was both (1) and (2); but what really irritated Colin was that the neighbours had no consideration for people around them, and indeed made the street look like a rough area. So in a way Colin's anger had more to do with his appraisal and judgement of the trigger, rather than the trigger itself. Nevertheless, if he wants to sort out his irritability and anger he needs to spot the 'visible' trigger of the boys playing football. Once he knows this is his weak spot, then he can sort out how to re-appraise it, if that is what he decides on.

If Colin wanted to become less irritated and angry, he could view the children playing outside in a different light. He could view it simply as 'kids having a good time' and 'showing that the street is a lively place to live'. Do you think that is likely to work with this man? No, neither did I.

So what is left? In this case, the main thing is to look in the response box. If you recollect, his response was to take the ball from the kids and storm round and shout at their mother. What other response do you think he might have made? Which of the following do you think would be best:

1 switch on the television, turn the volume up loud until their game is over;
2 every time the kids appear on the street, go round to their mother and put his point of view in as friendly a way as possible;
3 do nothing, just blank it all from his mind?

I would suggest that option (2) is the best one: to go round and put his point of view, amicably, just as often as he likes – preferably, from his point of view, just as soon as the kids appear on the street.

Many angry and irritable people make the mistake of thinking that the best reaction is (3), to 'do nothing at all'. This is not necessarily the case, particularly if you think that you are legitimately aggrieved. In such cases it is only right to stick up for your rights, assertively. But 'assertive' does not mean 'angry' or 'aggressive'.

So, in example (a), perhaps the best bet is for Colin to alter his response; and this is what he did. Nevertheless, the starting point was for him to be clear about what triggered his anger, rather than just thinking he was generally bad-tempered.

What about example (b), where five people, one at a time, came into the bar and left the door open behind them? They came at roughly 15–20-minute intervals and, finally, Steve got so angry that he confronted person number five.

So what was it that really triggered Steve's anger? There are several possibilities; which one do you think is most accurate:

1 the door being left open and the consequent cold draft;
2 the expression on the fifth man's face, being so self-centred and not caring about the cold air coming in;
3 Steve's perception that he was being made to look foolish, having to get up all the time to shut the door that somebody else had left open;
4 Steve's perception that he was not being given enough consideration by these other people?

Here, the literal trigger is (1), the door being left open and the ensuing blast of cold air. That – possibly in conjunction with the expression on the person's face – led to Steve's appraisal that he was being made to look foolish, that he was not being shown enough consideration.

So what could he have done to get rid of the trigger? (After all, getting rid of the trigger is normally what we want to do. If we can get rid of the trigger it stops the whole thing snowballing.) Which of the following would you recommend:

1 move to a different part of the bar, away from the door;
2 don't look at the person's face, so it doesn't annoy you;
3 realize that you are not being made a fool of;
4 don't worry about whether people are showing you consideration or not?

There is an argument in favour of each of these; which one(s) did you choose? Personally, I would go for number (1), even though it's not very 'psychological'. There are some things that most people would find irritating, and sitting by a door that people keep leaving open is probably one of them.

But what do you do, I hear you saying, if there are no other seats in the bar? In that case we have to look at the response. How did Steve actually respond? He jumped up and behaved in a threatening way to poor old person number five, having said nothing at all to the previous four people. So what might have been a better response? Maybe he should have just asked each person coming in to shut the door, in a non-aggressive way? We will look at this again later.

Now, you may have noticed that this bar example is rather different from the previous one. You may feel that there's more point in discussing the neighbour example, because that is an on-going situation which keeps happening every day or every week, and it's a good one to sort out a solution for. With the bar example, we seem to be harking back to something that's over and done with, so what's the point in going through it all over again?

The answer is that you can get so good at analyzing situations that you analyze them automatically, even as they're happening. So, whereas Steve may not find himself in an identical situation again, sitting right by a bar door that people keep leaving open, he may find himself in a somewhat similar one. In that case, if he has worked out a way of dealing with it, he will be able to analyze it even as it's going on and, hopefully, act in a better way.

What about example (c)? This was the case of Pam, who is so acutely annoyed by her husband when he eats noisily. Again, what do you think was the 'real' trigger for her annoyance:

1 the sheer decibel-level of her husband's eating – he should learn to eat more quietly;
2 the fact that he carried on talking to her while he was still chewing;
3 the fact that she saw it as symbolizing their incompatibility;
4 the fact that she had nothing better to do than worry about how much noise her husband made when he was eating?

Numbers (1) and (2) are the literal triggers. So how could we remove them? Earplugs to cut down the decibel-level won't help. Talk to him while he is chewing so that he isn't tempted to talk while chewing? Perhaps not.

Really, the problem lies in Pam's appraisal that the chewing symbolizes their incompatibility. So, ultimately, it is either that – or their incompatibility itself – that needs working on. Nevertheless, she does need to be clear on the initial trigger so that she can take action on it. In the interim she might also ask him to chew a bit more quietly. But that would probably be missing the point.

The next example, (d), involved Sue's teenage son Ian, who dropped a mug on the floor and broke it. Again, what was the trigger:

1 the mug breaking;
2 the cost of the mug;
3 the loud noise the mug made when it hit the floor;
4 Sue's appraisal that Ian is careless and needs to be taught a lesson?

Well, number (1) is obviously the 'literal' answer, but it is quickly followed by number (4). Clearly, once Sue knows what the triggers are for her thinking like that ('he is careless and needs to be taught a lesson') she can prepare a more helpful appraisal and train herself to use it at such times. (Such an appraisal might be: 'We all drop things on the floor from time to time, youngsters especially. There's no need to get uptight about it.')

So, what have we got so far, from looking at these first four examples?

- It is sometimes quite difficult to see exactly what the trigger is, because the 'literal' trigger and the appraisal are jumbled together.
- It is worthwhile disentangling these two aspects, because then you can prepare a more helpful appraisal if need be, and be ready to use it next time the trigger for your irritation and anger appears.
- Keeping a diary, on the model of Diary 1, is helpful in doing this.
- Often the key lies in learning a different response, for example tackling the neighbour in a different way, asking people to shut the door, tackling the under-lying issue of compatibility, telling the youngster to brush up the broken mug. But the same argument applies; before we can prepare a more helpful response, we need to be clear about what triggers our irritation and anger.

Let's move on now and have a look at the other examples.

The fifth one, (e), was about Alan, the electrician who was asked to do too much by his boss. What was the real trigger:

1 being overloaded with work;
2 feeling he is being put-upon by his boss?

Clearly the literal trigger is being overloaded with work. Feeling put-upon by his boss is the appraisal Alan makes.

In example (f) Anne lost her temper with her twelve-year-old daughter who was washing her hair in the bath.

What was the trigger for her anger:

1 the sight of her daughter in the bath;
2 the fact that her daughter hadn't tidied her bedroom;
3 the fact that she felt her daughter was being defiant;
4 the sense of frustration that she wasn't bringing her daughter up very well?

You will notice that a fourth option has crept in here that has got nothing to do with baths, tidy bedrooms or anything else. And this is sometimes the case. For example, some people will fight and argue simply because they are 'bored' or 'frustrated' or whatever. So in this case it is a possibility that Anne's anger has more to do with the frustration of wondering whether she is bringing her daughter up well than anything else.

In fact, frustration in general is frequently a trigger for anger or aggression, as was discovered by Miller and his colleagues back in the 1930s: a finding published as the 'frustration–aggression hypothesis'.

So what was your best answer as to what the trigger was for Anne? Possibly it was a mixture of frustration (partly to do with whether she is bringing her daughter up well, partly to do with her inability to get the girl to tidy her bedroom) and just seeing her daughter sitting in the bath when she wanted her to be doing something else. Her perception of 'defiance' is more an appraisal, following on from the trigger.

And our final example, (g), was to do with Ken, the stressed-out executive. What was the trigger for his irritability:

1 trying to cope with more work than he could reasonably do;
2 his colleague Phil being tactless;
3 just being in a bad mood that day?

From his account it sounds as though it was a combination of all three. Certainly he was overloaded with work, so he was in 'a bad mood'; but also perhaps the colleague was a shade tactless. Triggers can sometimes be slightly complex, as in 'my colleague being tactless when I'm overworked and in a bad mood'. Quite possibly none of the three elements mentioned (tactlessness, overwork, bad mood) would cause him to be irritable *on its own*.

Reading your diary (again)

The previous section will have got you pretty good at reading diaries in general – which means that you are also going to be pretty good at reading your own.

So all you have to do now is keep a diary of most of the times you get irritable and angry, along the lines described. Then analyze it to determine your triggers.

What you a looking for is a (short) list of triggers for

your irritation and anger. Here are some that other people
have produced:

- the neighbours playing loud music
- the kids next door playing football in the street
- the people next door showing no consideration for
  their neighbours
- other people being inconsiderate (as in the bar door)
- other people putting themselves above me (as in
  queue-jumping)
- my husband eating his food noisily
- my husband
- my wife
- my children
- my partner
- George, at work
- my son being careless
- being kept waiting
- being contradicted or proved wrong in public
- being overworked by my boss
- being dumped by my boyfriend
- my partner telling other people about things which
  were just between us
- my wife flirting with other men
- being made to look foolish in public
- my daughter being lazy
- my daughter being disobedient
- my son telling lies
- people stealing from me or damaging my property

- bouncers
- policemen
- being carved up by another driver
- being crammed in the tube
- being stressed out
- being bored
- being tired

SUMMARY

- It is important to have a very clear idea of what triggers your irritation and anger.
- Once you have that, you can either remove the trigger (although this is frequently impossible) or take a range of other actions, which we will cover later on.
- The best way of identifying what triggers your irritation and anger is to keep a diary; simply trying to recollect what triggers it is surprisingly unreliable. A good diary form for you to use (Diary 1) is included here.
- When you keep your diary you will find that you sometimes confuse triggers with appraisals (for example, writing the trigger down as 'half a dozen selfish so-and-so's down the bar' rather than 'half a dozen people coming in and leaving the door open'). Nevertheless, this can be helpful because, once you come to make you final (short) list of what triggers your anger, you may decide that the 'real' trigger is indeed 'other people's selfishness' rather than 'doors being left open'.
- A list of the triggers that other people have found for their anger is given above; this may be helpful as a starting point when compiling your own.

PROJECT

- Probably by keeping the diary (Diary 1), get a crystal clear idea of what triggers your irritation and anger. It may be specific (people leaving the lounge door open) or diffuse (my son being careless – which could be manifested in lots of ways), external (someone else doing something, e.g. dropping a mug on the floor) or internal (within you, e.g. being bored, being tired). However you do it, become an absolute expert on what makes you irritable or angry, so that if someone were to ask you, you could give them a vivid description of what does it for you.

- If possible, remove those triggers. You will find that this is surprisingly difficult. Some triggers can be removed, others cannot. Don't worry in either case. The following chapters will show you what to do if the trigger can't be removed. Nevertheless, if you can easily get rid of it, do so.

10

Why do I get angry?
1: Appraisal/judgement

What you will learn in this chapter

- The answer to the question posed in the chapter title: to put it more fully, 'Why do I always get irritated and angry at things that don't bother other people, and how do I sort it out?'
- The most common errors made in the appraisals and judgements people make of triggering situations.
- How to analyze some of the examples we have covered so far in terms of those common errors, so you get good at identifying such errors.
- How to make better appraisals and judgements and avoid the errors described.
- How to change your own behavior – permanently.

Why do I always get irritated and angry at things that don't bother other people?

We covered this earlier on, but just by way of revision:

- A potential trigger for anger occurs: e.g. you find your 12-year-old daughter in the bath washing her hair instead of tidying her room, having been asked to do so repeatedly.
- You make an appraisal/judgement of that situation which is likely to produce anger: e.g. 'She's deliberately being defiant, she's just trying to wind me up.' (It's worth noting at this stage that there is a possible alternative appraisal along the lines of 'Well, she's not tidying her room but at least she's keeping herself clean and tidy.')
- Assuming you made the anger-inducing appraisal, anger ensues.
- Your inhibitions may be strong enough to prevent the anger becoming apparent to anybody else.
- Or possibly your inhibitions are not that strong, so the potential recipient gets a piece of your mind: e.g. the daughter gets shouted at.

In Part One we summarized this process with the model shown again here in Figure 10.1.

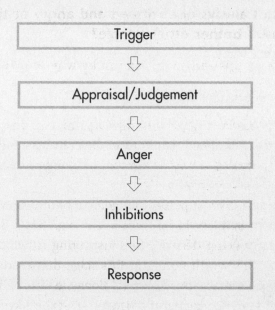

Figure 10.1 A model for analyzing irritability and anger

Appraising and judging in triggering situations: The most common errors

Happily, psychologists have completed a great deal of research into the kind of unhelpful appraisals that people make. And it turns out that such appraisals are not simply random: there are certain specific types of 'errors' that people tend to make. I've put the word 'errors' in quotes because while the appraisals may not necessarily be *wrong*, they are generally *unhelpful* to you. Read on and you will see what I mean.

A number of labels are given to the different categories of unhelpful appraisals that people make. Below are the ones that I think are the most important.

Selective perception

This means just what it sounds like: in other words, a person sees part of the story but not the whole story. For example, in the case of Anne's 12-year-old daughter sitting in the bath washing her hair, she was indeed 'not tidying her room' – but that was only part of the story. She was also keeping herself clean and tidy. In fact, as it turns out, this was particularly relevant because she was appearing in a school play the next morning, so it was relevant that she was 'well turned out'. However, to her mother's perception she was simply 'not tidying her room'.

Mind-reading

Again, this is exactly what it says. In our example it is manifested by Anne saying: 'She does it deliberately to wind me up.' How does she know her daughter does it to wind her up? The only possible answer can be by mind-reading. The point is that mind-reading is impossible, as far as we know. So Anne has no idea whether her daughter is really trying to wind her up deliberately or not. Therefore it is entirely unhelpful to jump to that conclusion. She might just as well jump to the opposite conclusion, that her daughter is *not* trying to wind her up deliberately. This is a very common way of thinking: many people assume that the person who irritates them does it deliberately.

Awfulizing

A clumsy word, but a good one for what it means. It refers to that phenomenon whereby, when we don't get what we want, we will see the situation as 'awful'. So, to take this example again, whereas some mothers, having failed to get their daughters to tidy their rooms, would tell somebody else: 'I wish I could get my daughter to tidy her room. Do you know I spent all day nagging her to do it yesterday and still she didn't do it,' other mothers will see it as 'awful' and 'the end of the world'. It is one example of 'thinking in extremes' or 'black and white thinking': seeing things as *either* wonderful *or* terrible, *either* perfect *or* awful, etc. It is good practice to develop the habit of thinking and talking in shades of grey, where, for example, events may be 'not as I want' but are not necessarily 'awful'.

Use of emotive language

Which is the particularly emotive word that Anne used about her 12-year-old daughter? The one that I would pick out is 'defiant'. She viewed her daughter as being deliberately defiant. This is a very strong word designed to make adversaries of mother and daughter. If one person defies another, then surely it is the first person's duty to overcome that defiance. This is likely to be a very unhelpful way of phrasing things.

Incidentally, although I am writing this as though we are talking out loud to somebody else, when we make our appraisals and judgements this is not normally the case; normally, the 'conversation' is with ourselves. That being the case, the language can be even more emotive. We can think nothing of referring to other people, even our own family, as 'bastards' and worse.

Overgeneralization

This is where we notice a particular observation which is true (e.g. that the girl in question has not tidied her room) and then make a sweeping generalization from that fact (e.g. 'She's bone idle' or 'She never does anything I ask her to'). It is usually far better to stick to the accurate statement, i.e. 'It is very difficult to get her to tidy her room.' This of course puts her on a par with just about every other youngster, and it also clarifies what the problem is (trying to get her to tidy her room). Overgeneralizations are very common and usually very destructive.

EXERCISE

These five types of errors in appraisal and judgement are very important. Therefore I would like you to stop reading for a moment and just look back over the five headings; then see if you can think of an example for each of the five where you have actually thought or reacted in the way described. In other words:

- an example of you showing selective perception (noticing only one aspect of a situation);
- an example of where you were 'mind-reading' (assuming you knew someone's intention when you could not possibly have done so);

- an example of 'awfulizing' (where you portrayed to yourself that what has happened is absolutely 'awful' rather than just 'not what you would have wished');
- an example of you using emotive language to yourself (describing an event in a way which is almost bound to get you 'fired up');
- an example of you 'overgeneralizing' (noticing something that is true, but going way over the top with a generalization from it).

However, take care not to blame yourself for any of these; all of them are very common indeed, but do tend to be rather unhelpful for you.

What errors of appraisal/judgement are being made here?

Below are a number of examples of triggers, along with the appraisal/judgement that was made by the recipient. After each example is a list of the five errors in appraisal/judgement. Your task is to <u>underline</u> all the errors which apply to each example (sadly, one appraisal can exhibit several of the errors). You may wish to circle the error which you think is the main one in each case.

The first three examples have been done for you:

1 *Trigger:* Gerry has noisy neighbours playing music loudly next door. This happens every week or so and normally lasts for an hour or two.

Gerry's appraisal: 'They do that deliberately to annoy me – they don't give a damn about what I think.'

Error(s): selective perception / <u>mind-reading</u> / awfulizing / <u>emotive language</u> / overgeneralizing.

2 *Trigger:* Colin's neighbours' kids are playing football in the street outside. This happens every few days and normally their game lasts for about forty-five minutes.

Colin's appraisal: 'They're a bloody nuisance, they've got no respect for anybody, it makes it not worth living here.'

Error(s): selective perception / mind-reading / <u>awfulizing</u> / <u>emotive language</u> / <u>overgeneralizing</u>.

3 *Trigger:* A fifth man comes into the bar where Steve is sitting with Ben and Chris and leaves a door open (four others having done so previously).

Steve's appraisal: 'They just don't give a damn about anybody.'

Error(s): selective perception / <u>mind-reading</u> / awfulizing / <u>emotive language</u> / <u>overgeneralizing</u>.

4 *Trigger:* Pam's husband eats food noisily and talks to her at the same time.

Pam's appraisal: 'I just can't stand the way he eats, it just shows how he's not my type of person.'

Error(s): selective perception / mind-reading / awfulizing / emotive language / overgeneralizing.

5 *Trigger:* Sue's teenage son Ian drops a china mug on the floor and it breaks. (Note: we know that Ian takes great care over his homework.)

Sue's appraisal: 'He doesn't take any care about anything, he just doesn't give a damn.'

Error(s): selective perception / mind-reading / awfulizing / emotive language / overgeneralizing.

6 *Trigger:* Judy has to wait a long time in the outpatient department with her five-year-old daughter. Having witnessed the doctor and nurse working carefully with a number of patients, she then sees them having a tea-break after an hour and a half, relaxing and chatting to each other.

Judy's appraisal: 'They don't care about any of us, all they are interested in doing is relaxing and flirting with each other.'

Error(s): selective perception / mind-reading / awfulizing / emotive language / overgeneralizing.

7 *Trigger:* Out at a party, Nigel's wife contradicts him several times in front of others.

Nigel's appraisal: 'She's doing it deliberately to show me up and make me look small – I just can't stand her any longer.'

Error(s): selective perception / mind-reading / awfulizing / emotive language / overgeneralizing.

8 *Trigger:* Alan's otherwise fair boss asks him to do another task towards the end of the day which will take him over his normal finishing time.

Alan's appraisal: 'He always treats me unfairly, he's just a lousy bastard.'

Error(s): selective perception / mind-reading / awfulizing / emotive language / overgeneralizing.

9 *Trigger:* Danny has told his long-time partner Vicky something he took to be in confidence. Vicky, however, has told several other people about this.

Danny's appraisal: 'That's totally out of order – she has got absolutely no sense of what's right and wrong.'

Error(s): selective perception / mind-reading / awfulizing / emotive language / overgeneralizing.

10 *Trigger:* Graham and Fiona have been married several years. Fiona has never had an extra-marital relationship and is generally a very good partner for Graham. However, she does sometimes flirt with other men.

Graham's appraisal: 'She's got no loyalty whatsoever; if I turned my back on her she'd be off like a shot.'

Error(s): selective perception / mind-reading / awfulizing / emotive language / overgeneralizing.

11 *Trigger:* Brian, standing at the bar, has his elbow jogged and beer spills down his front.

Brian's appraisal: 'He did that deliberately.'

Error(s): selective perception / mind-reading / awfulizing / emotive language / overgeneralizing.

12 *Trigger:* Paul's twelve-year-old son says that he has done his homework in order to get to watch television sooner.

Paul's appraisal: 'The kid's completely useless, I don't know what's going to happen if he carries on like this, he's going to do no good.'

Error(s): selective perception / mind-reading / awfulizing / emotive language / overgeneralizing.

13 *Trigger:* David sees a teenager stealing the stereo from the car.

David's appraisal: 'The kid was an animal, just thinks he can take what he wants, doesn't give a damn about anybody, the arrogant sod.'

Error(s): selective perception / mind-reading / awfulizing / emotive language / overgeneralizing.

14 *Trigger:* A bouncer outside a club speaks in a mildly irritated tone to a Tina, a twenty-year-old customer.

Tina's appraisal: 'Who does he think he is, these bloody bouncers think they own the place.'

Error(s): selective perception / mind-reading / awfulizing / emotive language / overgeneralizing.

15 *Trigger:* A car overtakes Chris's car and pulls in sharply in front of it in a line of traffic to avoid an oncoming car.

Chris's appraisal: 'Arrogant bastard, he only does that because he's got a Porsche, he's just trying to make everyone else look small.'

Error(s): selective perception / mind-reading / awfulizing / emotive language / overgeneralizing.

The answers I would give are as follows:

4 *Trigger:* Pam's husband eats food noisily and talks to her at the same time.

Pam's appraisal: 'I just can't stand the way he eats, it just shows how he's not my type of person.'

Error(s): selective perception / mind-reading / <u>awfulizing</u> / <u>emotive language</u> / (overgeneralizing.)

5 *Trigger:* Sue's teenage son Ian drops a china mug on the floor and it breaks. (Note: we know that Ian takes great care over his homework.)

Sue's appraisal: 'He doesn't take any care about anything, he just doesn't give a damn.'

Error(s): <u>selective perception</u> / mind-reading / <u>awfulizing</u> / <u>emotive language</u> / (overgeneralizing.)

6 *Trigger:* Judy has to wait a long time in the outpatient department with her five-year-old daughter. Having witnessed the doctor and nurse working carefully with a number of patients, she then sees them having a tea-break after an hour and a half, relaxing and chatting to each other.

Judy's appraisal: 'They don't care about any of us, all they are interested in doing is relaxing and flirting with each other.'

Error(s): <u>selective perception</u> / <u>mind-reading</u> / (awfulizing) / emotive language / overgeneralizing.

7 *Trigger:* Out at a party, Nigel's wife contradicts him several times in front of others.

Nigel's appraisal: 'She's doing it deliberately to show me up and make me look small – I just can't stand her any longer.'

Error(s): selective perception / <u>mind-reading</u> / <u>awfulizing</u> / emotive language / <u>overgeneralizing</u>.

8 *Trigger:* Alan's otherwise fair boss asks him to do another task towards the end of the day which will take him over his normal finishing time.

Alan's appraisal: 'He always treats me unfairly, he's just a lousy bastard.'

Error(s): <u>selective perception</u> / mind-reading / <u>awfulizing</u> / <u>emotive language</u> / <u>overgeneralizing</u>.

9 *Trigger:* Danny has told his long-time partner Vicky something he took to be in confidence. Vicky, however, has told several other people about this.

Danny's appraisal: 'That's totally out of order – she has got absolutely no sense of what's right and wrong.'

Error(s): <u>selective perception</u> / mind-reading / <u>awfulizing</u> / emotive language / <u>overgeneralizing</u>.

10 *Trigger:* Graham and Fiona have been married several years. Fiona has never had an extra-marital relationship and is generally a very good partner for Graham. However, she does sometimes flirt with other men.

Graham's appraisal: 'She's got no loyalty whatsoever; if I turned my back on her she'd be off like a shot.'

Error(s): <u>selective perception</u> / <u>mind-reading</u> / awfulizing / emotive language / overgeneralizing.

11 *Trigger:* Brian, standing at the bar, has his elbow jogged and beer spills down his front.

Brian's appraisal: 'He did that deliberately.'

Error(s): selective perception / <u>mind-reading</u> / awfulizing / emotive language / overgeneralizing.

12 *Trigger:* Paul's 12-year-old son says that he has done his homework in order to get to watch television sooner.

Paul's appraisal: 'The kid's completely useless, I don't know what's going to happen if he carries on like this, he's going to do no good.'

Error(s): <u>selective perception</u> / mind-reading / <u>awfulizing</u> / <u>emotive language</u> / <u>overgeneralizing</u>.

13 *Trigger:* David sees a teenager stealing the stereo from the car.

David's appraisal: 'The kid was an animal, just thinks he can take what he wants, doesn't give a damn about anybody, the arrogant sod.'

Error(s): selective perception / <u>mind-reading</u> / awfulizing / <u>emotive language</u> / <u>overgeneralizing</u>.

14 *Trigger:* A bouncer outside a club speaks in a mildly irritated tone to a Tina, a 20-year-old customer.

Tina's appraisal: 'Who does he think he is, these bloody bouncers think they own the place.'

Error(s): selective perception / <u>mind-reading</u> / <u>awfulizing</u> / emotive language / overgeneralizing.

15 *Trigger:* A car overtakes Chris's car and pulls in sharply in front of it in a line of traffic to avoid an oncoming car.

Chris's appraisal: 'Arrogant bastard, he only does that because he's got a Porsche, he's just trying to make everyone else look small.'

Error(s): selective perception / <u>mind-reading</u> / awfulizing / <u>emotive language</u> / overgeneralizing.

SUMMARY OF THE MAIN APPRAISAL/ JUDGEMENT ERRORS

- Selective perception: Where one or more important aspects of the situation are unnoticed.
- Mind-reading: Where a person believes s/he knows what is in another person's mind, especially their intention.
- Awfulizing: Where some unwanted event is viewed as awful, tragic, terrible, disastrous, etc., rather than simply unwelcome.
- Emotive language: Using strong language to oneself, almost automatically producing an angry reaction.
- Overgeneralization: Making a sweeping generalization from one true observation.

Applying this to your own situation

Now you've shown you can analyze other examples, you need some examples from your own life to work on. To get these, we need a slightly more sophisticated diary, as shown opposite.

Diary 2

Fill this in as soon as possible after each time you get irritable or angry.

Trigger: Describe here what a video camera would have seen or heard. Include the day and date, but do not put what you thought or how you reacted.

_____

_____

_____

Appraisal/Judgement: Write here the thoughts that went through your mind, as clearly as you can remember them.

_____

_____

_____

Anger: Leave this blank for the time being.

_____

_____

Inhibitions: Leave this blank for the time being.

_____

_____

_____

Response: Write here what a video camera would have seen you do and heard you say, as clearly as you can.

_____

_____

_____

More helpful appraisal/judgement: How else might you have appraised the situation? To determine this, you might like to consider the following: What errors are you making (selective perception, mind-reading, awfulizing, emotive language, over-generalization)?

If you had an all-knowing, all-wise friend, how would s/he have seen the situation?

Is a reframing of the situation possible? (A glass that is half empty is also half full.)

What would your cost–benefit analysis be of seeing the situation the way you did?

Methods of making your appraisals/judgements more helpful

There are four major ways of doing this.

Identify and remove 'errors' of judgement

This starts with analyzing your appraisal/judgement. So, for example, Anne, who saw her daughter 'not tidying her room', might realize that this was selective perception. In other words, while it was true the girl was not tidying her room, she *was* washing her hair and thereby making herself clean and tidy for the next morning's school play. This positive aspect of the girl's behavior was something that had completely eluded Anne. She had truly only perceived the fact that her daughter was not tidying her room. Once this 'error' had been spotted, the situation almost automatically rectified itself.

In the same way, Anne might also see that she was 'mind-reading', another 'error'. In this instance she was saying to herself that her daughter was 'deliberately winding her up'. Clearly this is mind-reading; how could the mother possibly know that the daughter had that intention? Once this has been spotted as an 'error', Anne believed it less firmly.

She also recognized that she was 'awfulizing'. In other words, she was making the fact that her daughter had not tidied her room into the 'biggest thing in the world' – in her own words, 'getting it out of proportion'.

She was also using emotive language, describing her daughter as 'defiant'. This is a strong word which produces strong emotional reactions. What is more, it is also mind-reading: it implies that Anne can tell that the daughter has a particular motive in mind. The 'error' of using emotive language is easily corrected – you simply refrain from using it. You simply delete from your mind the phrase where the word 'defiant' was used.

And the final error is over-generalization: in this instance, saying that the daughter was 'bone idle'. This was not actually true: there are all sorts of other things that the daughter did perfectly well (for example, keeping herself clean and tidy, joining in the school play, etc.). Again, in this instance once the 'error' has been spotted, the situation almost automatically corrects itself.

It is perhaps worth making the point that there are rather few examples that illustrate all five errors simultaneously, and that is why this episode of Anne and her daughter is something of a 'collectors' item'!

The 'friend technique'

This is where you say to yourself: If I had an all-knowing, all-wise friend, someone who had only my interests at heart, how would s/he appraise this situation so that it worked out best for me?

In this instance the friend might say something like 'Come on, Anne, just leave the girl alone. She's a good girl, and at least she's keeping herself clean and tidy which is a step ahead of a lot of kids. Anyway, how many kids do you know who tidy their rooms when their mums ask them to?'

This can be a powerful technique if you practice it regularly and if you can build up a good image of this all-knowing, all-wise friend. It does not have to be anybody real – perhaps it's helpful if it isn't – just so long as it is a very wise person who has your interests at heart, someone who is always on your side.

Incidentally, some people prefer to do it the other way around: in other words, ask themselves: 'What would you say to a friend in this situation, a really good friend to whom you wanted to offer constructive support?'

Reframing the trigger

Most 'bad news' can also be reframed as 'good news'. The most famous example is the glass of water that is half empty (bad news). It is of course also half full (good news).

So how might you reframe the situation where, in spite of being nagged all day long, your 12-year-old daughter is sitting in the bath washing her hair rather than tidying her room? There are in fact several options here. One is to simply focus on the good aspect, the 'half full' aspect: namely, in this case, the fact that she is keeping herself clean and tidy and preparing for the school play. Another is that clearly the daughter feels relaxed enough with her mother, and 'un-frightened' enough of her, not to feel that she has to do exactly what she's told. This 'quality of relationship' aspect is normally viewed as good news and would not usually produce anger. A third possible reframe is that in fact the daughter is displaying assertiveness and perseverance by not simply doing what she is told. Both these characteristics are rightly viewed as good qualities to encourage in youngsters.

Some situations are much more difficult to reframe. Take the example of Steve, where every other person who comes into the bar leaves the door open: how might that be reframed? It is very difficult to see anything intrinsically good about people leaving the door open just near where you are sitting. On the other hand, if you look at the situation in a much wider perspective, maybe it is just possible. The overall situation is, after all, that there you are sitting with two friends having a good drink and a talk and occasionally somebody leaves the door open. Supposing you were to have a conversation with some chap who had just lost all he owned in an earthquake in Turkey, or a man who had lost his loved ones in the floods in Bangladesh, or a woman who had lost everything and everybody in a natural catastrophe in South America. Suppose you were to suggest to this individual that there is a chap sitting in a bar drinking happily with his two friends who views it as a disaster when several people leave the door open by him. What sort of reaction would you be likely to get?

That, strictly speaking, is reframing: it puts the event in a different context. And it might just sway the person concerned; you might just be able to use it. Curiously, though, my experience is that it *doesn't* often do the trick. Only when there is real personal relevance (as in the first example of seeing the 12-year-old daughter as 'a good kid looking after herself and getting ready for the play at school next day') do people really latch onto it. Nevertheless, I mentioned the second example of reframing because it is one that works well for me personally; so, who knows, it might work for you too.

Cost–benefit analysis

Doing a cost–benefit analysis of your appraisal/judgement is, happily, not half so difficult as it sounds. It's really just a matter of looking at the pros and cons.

For consistency's sake it would probably be a good idea to stick to just one example for the most part while we go through these options, namely our mother Anne with her 12-year-old daughter. But I'm getting a bit fed up with that example, so let's look instead at Paul, the father with the son, also aged 12, who hadn't done his homework properly but said he had so he could watch the television. When Paul had a look at the homework and saw how little had been done his appraisal was something like this: 'The boy's a liar, he's tried to pull the wool over my eyes, where's he going to get to if he carries on like this? He'll come to no good in life, all the other kids at school will do better than him . . .'

Clearly this is a piece of selective perception in that there are probably other aspects to the boy that we haven't been told about; his life cannot begin and end with that one piece of undone homework. Nevertheless, the father's appraisal/judgement may indeed turn out to be correct. The only thing is, we would have to wait for a number of years before we would find out one way or the other. And even then it might only be correct because it was a self-fulfilling prophecy.

In the meantime, what are the pros and cons of making an appraisal/judgement like that? Let's do the cons (against) first:

- it agitates the father;
- it makes the boy feel inadequate;
- it worsens the relationship between father and son;
- it labels school work as a thoroughly punishing business . . .

. . . and there are probably more cons that you can think of. On the 'pro' side there's – well, precious little that I can imagine. Possibly it might motivate the son to do more homework next time; but then again, it might motivate him to be a bit more devious next time so he can get away with it.

What about an appraisal/judgement along the lines of: 'The kid has clearly got no idea what he's doing, I'd better see if I can help him out or see if he knows somebody else who can if I can't'? Clearly the cost–benefit analysis in this case swings right round the other way. The benefits of such an appraisal are:

- an improvement in the father–son relationship;
- better school work;
- probably more openness about how things are going . . .

. . . and so on. The costs are probably significant too: predominantly, a drain on the father's time. On balance, however, the second appraisal/judgement produces a much better cost–benefit analysis for all concerned than the first one.

Now, if you're like anybody else, you may say that you can't decide how to think on the basis of a cost–benefit analysis; you think according to what is 'true'. Well, maybe; but I would tend to disagree, because we've seen that it is very difficult to see what is 'true' in this instance – and indeed in many others. And moreover, if you look at how people do think, even down to something as tangible as which political party to vote for, it very often is to do with what would benefit them the most and cost them the least.

THE MAIN METHODS OF PRODUCING MORE HELPFUL APPRAISALS/JUDGEMENTS

- Identify the error (selective perception, mind-reading, awfulizing, emotive language or overgeneralisation) and correct it.
- The 'friend technique'. How would an all-knowing, all-wise friend advise you to view the situation?
- Reframe the situation. Search for the good aspects of it, or, failing that, view it from a completely different perspective.
- Conduct a cost–benefit analysis. That is, examine the costs and benefits of appraising the situation the way you are, and then look for a more cost-effective way.

EXERCISE

Graham's wife, Fiona, occasionally indulges in 'harmless flirting' with other men – merely in high spirits, with no intention of getting involved in an extra-marital relationship. Graham, however, gets very jealous and produces an appraisal/judgement along the lines of: 'She's showing me up, people will think I'm not making her happy, I'm losing face, she's out of order.'

1 What alternative appraisal would an all-knowing, all-wise friend make?
2 How might Graham reframe this behavior?
3 What would a cost–benefit analysis of Graham's appraisal look like? Can you suggest a better appraisal?

Below are the kind of answers that I produced, but I would strongly suggest that you produce your own before you have a look at these:

1 A reassuring friend might say: 'Come on, Graham, you know perfectly well that Fiona is as faithful as the day is long, she'd never let you down, she thinks you're the best thing since sliced bread. She just likes to have lots of fun but everybody knows what she thinks of you.'

2 Graham might reframe the situation as: 'It's good that Fiona feels secure enough in our relationship that she can have a great time and know that I won't take it amiss and neither would anybody else.'

3 A cost–benefit analysis of Graham's original appraisal/judgement is that the 'costs' are rather heavy: his appraisal will make him anxious, jealous and possibly angry. It will put a strain on the relationship, it will limit Fiona's activities, make her feel that Graham doesn't trust her and generally put a damper on all their activities. The only benefit of such an appraisal is that at least it lets Fiona know that Graham cares about her – but she probably knows that anyway. Yes, a better appraisal would be along the lines of (1) or (2) above.

Let's look at another example ...

EXERCISE

Vicky, while being interviewed on a radio programme, mentioned that her husband Danny likes to wear her thongs. Danny, who is also in the public eye, took a very dim view of this, making an appraisal/judgement along the lines of: 'Has she got no sense? Doesn't she realize that some things are just between us? Is she deliberately trying to make my life as difficult as possible? She's just completely stupid!' Needless to say, this made Danny very angry with Vicky.

1 What error of thinking was Danny making?
2 What alternative appraisal would an all-knowing, all-wise friend make?
3 How might Danny reframe what Vicky did?
4 What would a cost–benefit analysis of Danny's appraisal look like? Can you suggest a better appraisal?

Again, there is a list of answers that I would make below, but I would suggest that you produce your own before you have a look at these.

1 Danny is making a lot of thinking errors. Particularly, he is using emotive language ('she's completely stupid') and over-generalizing (just because she has said one thing – or even several things – which would be best left unsaid, it does not mean that she is completely stupid; probably there are lots of other things which would suggest she is far from stupid). One might also say that Danny is mind-reading (assuming that Vicky is trying to make his life as difficult as possible). Likewise, you could say that he is indulging in selective perception (because Vicky probably does other things which make his life good) and you might even say he is awfulizing (is it really so bad that people know that he and his wife have an intimate side to their relationship?).

2 An all-knowing, all-wise friend might say 'Oh, look, Danny, there's no need to make quite such a big deal out of it. You know that Vicky thinks the world of you and wouldn't deliberately do things to make things difficult for you. So what if other people rib you a bit? It only shows that they're jealous. Just put it to one side.'

3 How might Danny reframe what Vicky said and did? He might say that it is good that Vicky feels so relaxed and secure in their relationship that she doesn't have to watch every word she says, even when she's being interviewed on nationwide radio. He might even say that it adds to his street-cred that he has a pretty adventurous private life as well as the public one that most people see. He could even relish the fact that other people are made jealous by what she said.

4 A cost–benefit analysis would look something like this. The costs of the appraisal that Danny is making originally are heavy: it puts a strain on his relationship with Vicky, it makes him feel stressed out in general, it makes him angry with Vicky. The benefits are few: possibly it might make Vicky a bit more cautious about what she says in future, but does Danny really want her to be nervous about everything she says? A better appraisal would be something like the 'best friend' said in (2) above. That would have lots of benefits for Danny and no costs.

And another one ...

When thirteen-year-old Ian accidentally dropped a mug on the kitchen floor and it broke, his mother Sue 'completely lost it'. Her appraisal was that 'The kid is spoiled to death, he just doesn't realize that things cost money, he just doesn't give a damn. He thinks I'll clear up after him, buy everything that's necessary and just act as his slave. Well, it's about time he learned a lesson.' Again,

1 What errors in thinking is Sue making?
2 What alternative appraisal would an all-knowing, all-wise friend suggest?
3 How might Sue reframe what Ian did?
4 What would a cost-benefit analysis of Sue's appraisal look like? Can you suggest a better appraisal?

And again you are probably best to work the answers out yourself before going on to read the ones below.

1 Sue is using emotive language ('he doesn't give a damn, he thinks I'll act like his slave, it's about time he learned a lesson'), she is mind-reading (how does she know he doesn't give a damn?) and she is probably overgeneralizing (just because he drops the occasional mug it doesn't mean he doesn't care about things or that he sees his mother as a slave).

2 An all-knowing, all-wise friend might say 'Listen, Sue, how much does a mug cost? And is it really that difficult to sweep up a broken mug? In any case, you could get him to do that, and that would probably be the best way of him 'learning a lesson', as you put it. Now, just calm yourself down and get him to clear up the bits.'

3 Possibly Sue might reframe the incident as another small part of Ian's development, in that he learns that when you make a mistake, even a small one, like breaking a mug, you have to rectify it – in this case, sweep up the pieces. Or she could look at it from a completely different perspective: she could take the view of one of the millions of people in the world whose lives are seriously at risk on a daily basis and then ask herself how one such person would perceive the breaking of a mug that was easily replaced.

4 A cost–benefit analysis of Sue's appraisal would be that the costs to her are heavy: she is stressed-out, agitated, angry with Ian and wearing down the relationship between them. The benefits of such an appraisal are slim: possibly Ian might be somewhat more careful next time, but equally possible he may be so nervous next time he is in the kitchen with his mum that he is *more* likely to drop something; or perhaps he might not even risk making himself a drink when she's about, so she would see less of him around the house. Again, a better appraisal would be that of the best friend or even possible that [in (3) above] of a person whose life is constantly at risk on a daily basis, i.e. 'a broken mug is nothing to worry about.'

So how do you change really, permanently?

The RCR technique

RCR stands for *Review, Cement, Record*. And each of these is very important.

Reviewing means you examine events that happen to you (and especially events when you have felt angry and irritable) in exactly the same way as we have done in the three exercises we have just looked at. In other words, you actually write down what happened to you in exactly the same way as in each of these exercises. The description can be quite brief; it need only take up a few lines. Importantly, though, it does contain both the event and your appraisal of it – just like the three examples in the exercises. And again, just as in the exercises, you take yourself through the four stages of analysis. Use Diary 2 if you want.

The purpose of this is for you to form a judgement as to how you should best view the event. Now, you might say that you can't *decide* how to view an event – an event happens and your appraisal/judgement appears in a flash and is therefore the true one. A lot of us feel this; but I'm afraid it is the thinking of a five-year-old: 'Because I see it this way it *is* this way.' Not at all. Events happen, and there are as many different ways of seeing them as there are people in the world. What you have to do is to come to a judgement as to your best way of seeing it, the way that is in your best interests.

This can be tricky, because by now you will certainly be well into the habit of seeing things in particular ways, and changing those ways is quite a task. Rather like finding your way through a jungle, it is always easier to take the already existing paths. However, it is unfortunate for you if those paths happen to be 'the awfulizing path', 'the emotive language path', 'the mind-reading path' and so on.

There is some good news, though: as far as the brain is concerned it doesn't really matter much whether you do things in reality or in imagination. What this means is that simply reviewing things in the way I have just described, taking yourself through the four stages of analysis, and simply *imagining* thinking in the most cost-effective way is almost as good as actually doing it at the time of the event – in terms of changing your patterns of thinking. Nevertheless, you do have to do it lots of times. Effectively, you are beating a new path through the jungle of the brain;

and you have to keep treading down that path to make it a viable route. So keep reviewing, keep taking yourself through the four stages, and keep settling on the most cost-effective appraisal.

(For those of you who watch cricket, you will sometimes see a batsman rehearsing the stroke *he should have played*. On the face of it this seems a pretty daft thing to do, as the ball has just gone whistling past him and he played a rather poorer stroke than the one he is now rehearsing. Not so, however: that rehearsal he is now doing is in fact treading down a better path through the jungle of the brain. The next time a cricket ball comes hurtling towards him in similar fashion there is a better chance that he will take that new improved path rather than the previous faulty one. For those of you who are not interested in cricket, you must wonder what on earth I am going on about. Don't worry. Think jungle.)

Cementing is equally important. Just as it's impossible to distinguish between the relative importance of brakes and steering on a car, so with reviewing and cementing. They are both essential.

What you do with cementing is to act out the appraisal you settled on during the review stage. In other words, thinking something is not enough; you actually have to *behave* that way. I call it cementing because it figuratively cements, fixes, the thoughts you have produced. Thoughts and behavior make a very strong combination – indeed, this is the key combination that underlies a cognitive behavioral approach to solving problems.

So, in the examples given in the exercises above, Graham must 'act out' being pleased that Fiona feels secure enough in the relationship that she can have a great time by flirting with other men. This is more than simply pretending, because by now Graham really has reframed the situation and has got his new cost-effective appraisal; so it is a question of 'acting out what he thinks' rather than pretending. In other words, he would joke with Fiona about it all afterwards, might tease her about it while it is going on, and so on.

Likewise, Danny will genuinely act out his new more cost-effective appraisal to the slip-ups that Vicky makes. So he can tease her about how her mouth runs away with her, the new perception that other people have of him, and so forth.

Sue, too, will cement her new appraisal by *calmly* asking Ian to sweep up the remnants of the mug, in due course *calmly* buy a replacement mug or two, and so on.

Importantly, this need not just be retrospective. Graham can be sure that he reacts this way to *future* flirting episodes from Fiona; Danny can be sure he reacts this way to *future* misjudged comments from Vicky; and Sue should ensure that she reacts this way to *future* 'careless acts' from Ian.

Recording is the part where you reap the pay-off: now you can simply enjoy feeling extra smug. All you do is write down a brief account of events as they happen; so, the next time Fiona does some of her flirting, Graham writes down a brief account of it, what his (new, improved) appraisal was, and how he reacted during and after the event. And this will make good reading for him because it will be such an improvement on his previous responses. Again, he could use Diary 2 if he wanted.

Likewise, Danny will simply make a brief note about Vicky's latest gaffe, what his new, improved appraisal was, and how he reacted during it and afterwards. And Sue will do just the same, keeping an account of the things that Ian gets up to, her new appraisals and her new reactions.

So the recording stage is clearly the most fun and enables you to see that your hard work is paying off in a good way: not just that those around you are not having to suffer your irritability and anger, but that you are genuinely seeing things in a different light, one which is more beneficial for you too.

SUMMARY

- The reason why you get irritated and angry at things that don't seem to bother other people is that you make different appraisals and judgements about those events.
- The most common errors made in appraising and judging situations are selective perception, mind-reading, awfulizing, using emotive language and overgeneralization.
- It is straightforward – with lots of practice – to analyze examples and see the errors that are being made.
- It is possible to make appraisals and judgements that are better for all concerned, making both you and other people feel better about the situation. The main ways of doing this are: (a) identify the error and correct it, (b) the 'friend technique' (how will an all-knowing, all-wise friend advise you to view the situation?), (c) reframe the situation by searching for good

aspects of it or viewing it from a completely different perspective, and (d) conduct a cost–benefit analysis, examining the costs and benefits of appraising the situation the way you are doing and then looking for a more cost effective way.

• You can bring about a permanent change in your own behavior by the RCR technique. This means *reviewing* events as they crop up and conducting the four-stage analysis to produce more helpful appraisals and judgements, *cementing* this new, more cost-effective appraisal by behaving in a way that matches it, then *recording* the results to further consolidate the gains and generally make you feel good about your progress.

PROJECT

The best project you can do to apply this chapter to your own situation and thereby change your own behavior is as follows:

• Keep a record of events that trigger your anger and, most importantly, what your appraisal of those events is. Use Diary 2 if you want.

• Analyze your appraisals and produce better, more helpful, more cost-effective ones. A brief account of how to do this is contained in the fourth point of the summary above.

• Cement your new appraisals by acting in line with them. This is a strong technique where your thoughts and behavior support each other.

• It is a good idea also to record in writing what you have just done (the trigger, your new appraisal, how you cemented that new appraisal); this cements things even further.

11

Why do I get angry? 2: Beliefs

We covered a great deal of ground in the previous chapter, and if you have acted on it you will already have made a terrific impact on your own irritability and anger. Nevertheless, there is a question that might have occurred to you, and it is a question that can appear in several forms, as follows:

- Why is it always *me* who makes these unhelpful appraisals and judgements, rather than my friend John, Kate or whoever?
- Why was it Steve who got angry about the guy who came into the bar and left the door open, rather than Ben or Chris?
- Why was it that Sue made the unhelpful appraisal/judgement when her teenage son dropped her mug on the floor, whereas other mothers don't make such unhelpful appraisals?
- Why did Anne make such an unhelpful appraisal of her twelve-year-old who was washing her hair

in the bath (not tidying her room) while some other mothers wouldn't?

- Why is it that when Chris is 'cut off' by another motorist, he makes an appraisal that gets him really angry, whereas other motorists will just shrug it off?

Of course, these are all simply different forms of the same question: namely, why are some people 'set up' to make unhelpful appraisals whereas other people seem to be 'set up' to make helpful appraisals?

Again, we talked about this in Part One; in this chapter we will look at how to remedy the situation. If you are someone who is prone to make unhelpful appraisals, appraisals which lead you to be irritable and angry quite often, then this is your chance to reprogramme yourself. And, perhaps surprisingly, it's not too difficult; in fact, it can be quite a lot of fun.

Let's go back to our model. We can see from the diagram that the way we appraise things is influenced partly by our beliefs. We've shaded that box in because that's the box we're going to focus on in this chapter. We are going to look at how those beliefs influence the way we appraise things and how we can alter those beliefs; because if we can do that, then we will automatically alter our appraisals without any further effort. We will, effectively, be a significantly different person, someone who is fundamentally less prone to be irritable and angry.

You can see from the diagram on page 144 that by changing the beliefs we will change the whole course of events.

Incidentally, you might be thinking that it's not so much that you are *always* prone to make unhelpful appraisals, it's just that *sometimes* you are. Particularly when you just 'feel irritable'. In that case, Chapter 15 on 'mood' is going to be particularly relevant to you. Even so, if you are wondering whether it's worth your while reading this chapter (and all the others between here and Chapter 15) then I would suggest that the most likely answer is: 'Yes, it is.' This one in particular is just such a good chapter! It looks at things which are absolutely fundamental and yet relatively easy to change. So, potentially there is a big pay-off for little effort, and pleasurable effort at that.

What sort of beliefs are we talking about?

What we are dealing with here are beliefs about yourself, about other people, about the nature of the world, about how things should be, about how life is to be lived, and so on. We are *not* concerned with beliefs on matters of fact (as in, I believe it is about 3,500 miles from London to New York, or I believe the capital of Australia is Camberra).

A lot has been written about the beliefs that people hold and how helpful or otherwise they are. People have made lists of unhelpful beliefs – beliefs that make you anxious, beliefs that make you depressed, and so forth. In my experience, having read lots of lists and seen lots of irritable and angry people, my own list of unhelpful beliefs is as follows:

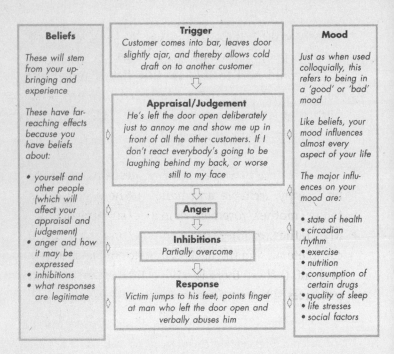

Figure 11.1 A model for analyzing irritability and anger

- Things should be just exactly how I want them to be. It is awful if they are not.
- People don't take any notice of you unless you show that you are irritated or angry. It is the only way of making your point.
- Other people are basically selfish, self-centred and unhelpful. If you want them to help you, you have to *make* them.
- Other people are basically hostile. You have to be on the alert, otherwise they will take any opportunity to put you down.

- If people do wrong they must be punished. You can't let people get way with things.

  We could add to this another list of unhelpful beliefs which are a bit more specific, referring to particular situations or particular people:
- It's okay to get angry with/hit policemen, bouncers, etc.
- A parent/foreman/manager/supervisor is *meant* to be snappy, irritable and harsh. (Where you are a father/mother/foreman/manager/supervisor).
- My father/mother/partner/son/daughter is a complete pain in the neck, it irritates me just to look at them. (Where there is one particular person who produces that emotional reaction in you.)

Exercise

Let's have a look at the basic list of five unhelpful beliefs. In each of the following examples, underline the answer which you think is best. In some cases there may be more than one possibility, in those cases underline more than one. The first two have been completed for you.

1 Steve, Ben and Chris are all sitting in a bar, near to the door. During the course of the evening four people come in and leave the door open. When the fifth person comes in it is Steve who gets angry.

This is because Steve believes that things should be just how he wants them / **believes people take no notice unless**

you are irritated or angry / **believes people are selfish, self-centred and unhelpful** / believes people are hostile and constantly trying to put you down / believes if people do wrong they must be punished, you can't let people get way with things.

2 In a particular street in a medium-sized town there are seventeen mothers who have youngsters between the ages of 5 and 15. All those youngsters, to a greater or lesser degree, drop mugs on the floor from time to time.

Sue gets much angrier than any of the other sixteen because **she believes that things should be just how she wants them** / **believes people take no notice unless you are irritated or angry** / believes people are selfish, self-centred and unhelpful / believes people are hostile and constantly trying to put you down / believes if people do wrong they must be punished, you can't let people get way with things.

3 Nigel's wife has a habit of contradicting him when they are out in public. This makes him very angry because he feels he 'loses face' in front of other people.

This is because he basically believes that things should be just how he wants them / believes people take no notice unless you are irritated or angry / believes people are selfish, self-centred and unhelpful / believes people are hostile and constantly trying to put you down / believes if people do wrong they must be punished, you can't let people get way with things.

4 Alan, the electrician, feels really 'put upon' and angry when his boss asks him to do extra tasks towards the end of the day.

He tends to see his boss in this light because he basically believes that things should be just how he wants them / believes people take no notice unless you are irritated or angry / believes people are selfish, self-centred and unhelpful / believes people are hostile and constantly trying to put you down / believes if people do wrong they must be punished, you can't let people get way with things.

5 When Fiona flirts with other men it makes her husband, Graham, very angry. On the other hand, when Hannah flirts with other men, her husband Ian does not get angry.

The difference between the two men is that Graham basically believes that things should be just how he wants them / believes people take no notice unless you are irritated or angry / believes people are selfish, self-centred and unhelpful / believes people are hostile and constantly trying to put you down believes if people do wrong they must be punished, you can't let people get way with things.

6 One evening in November 1999 a total of around one million people drank in a British pub. Of that one million people, about 10,000 were jogged so that they spilt their drink over themselves. Of those 10,000, Brian was the only one who broke a beer mug and pushed it in the face of the person who jogged him.

Part of the reason he reacted so badly is that he believes that things should be just how he wants them / believes people take no notice unless you are irritated or angry / believes people are selfish, self-centred and unhelpful / believes people are hostile and constantly trying to put you down / believes if people do wrong they must be punished, you can't let people get way with things.

7 On a particular estate in a particular city there are around 600 children between the ages of five and fifteen. Only about fifty of them keep their rooms tidy enough to satisfy their parents. Most parents on this estate nag their children to keep their rooms tidier. Anne, on the other hand, completely 'loses her cool' with her twelve-year-old daughter.

This is because Anne believes that things should be just how she wants them / believes people take no notice unless you are irritated or angry / believes people are selfish, self-centred and unhelpful / believes people are hostile and constantly trying to put you down / believes if people do wrong they must be punished, you can't let people get way with things.

8 Paul feels terrible because he hit his twelve year-old son across the face because the boy hadn't done his homework and had lied to him about it.

However, Paul was prone to react this way because deep down he believes that things should be just how he wants them / believes people take no notice unless you are irritated or angry / believes people are selfish, self-centred and unhelpful / believes people are hostile and constantly trying to put you down / believes if people do wrong they must be punished, you can't let people get way with things.

9 Another driver cut across Chris' path as he was going round a roundabout. He got so angry that he 'tailgated' the other driver for five miles. Eventually, the other driver got out and confronted Chris, and there was a fight during which Chris came off very much second best.

Chris would never have behaved this way in the first place had he not believed that things should be just how he wants them / believed people take no notice unless you are irritated or angry / believed people are selfish, self-centred and unhelpful / believed people are hostile and constantly trying to put you down / believed if people do wrong they must be punished, you can't let people get way with things.

How did you get on? Below is the same list of my own answers. Some of them are certainly debatable, but at least they will give you food for thought.

1 Steve, Ben and Chris are all sitting in a bar, near to the door. During the course of the evening four people come in and leave the door open. When the fifth person comes in it is Steve who gets angry.

This is because Steve believes that things should be just how he wants them / believes people take no notice unless you are irritated or angry / **believes people are selfish, self-centred and unhelpful** / believes people are hostile and constantly trying to put you down / **believes if people do wrong they must be punished, you can't let people get way with things.**

2 In a particular street in a medium-sized town there are seventeen mothers who have youngsters between the ages of five and fifteen. All those youngsters, to a greater or lesser degree, drop mugs on the floor from time to time.

Sue gets much angrier than any of the other sixteen because **she believes that things should be just how she wants them** / **believes people take no notice unless you are irritated or angry** / believes people are selfish, self-centred and unhelpful / believes people are hostile and constantly trying to put you down / believes if people do wrong they must be punished, you can't let people get way with things.

3 Nigel's wife has a habit of contradicting him when they are out in public. This makes him very angry because he feels he 'loses face' in front of other people.

This is because he basically believes that things should be just how he wants them / believes people take no notice unless you are irritated or angry / believes people are selfish, self-centred and unhelpful / **believes people are hostile and constantly trying to put you down** / believes if people do wrong they must be punished, you can't let people get way with things.

4 Alan, the electrician, feels really 'put upon' and angry when his boss asks him to do extra tasks towards the end of the day.

He tends to see his boss in this light because he basically believes that things should be just how he wants them / believes people take no notice unless you are irritated or angry / **believes people are selfish, self-centred and unhelpful** / believes people are hostile and constantly trying to put you down / believes if people do wrong they must be punished, you can't let people get way with things.

5 When Fiona flirts with other men it makes her husband, Graham, very angry. On the other hand, when Hannah flirts with other men, her husband Ian does not get angry.

The difference between the two men is that Graham basically **believes that things should be just how he wants them** / believes people take no notice unless you are irritated or angry / believes people are selfish, self-centred and unhelpful / **believes people are hostile and constantly trying to put you down** / believes if people do wrong they must be punished, you can't let people get way with things.

6 One evening in November 1999 a total of around one million people drank in a British pub. Of that one million people about 10,000 were jogged so that they spilt their drink over them. Of those 10,000, Brian was the only one who broke a beer mug and pushed it in the face of the person who jogged him.

Part of the reason he reacted so badly is that he believes that things should be just how he wants them / believes people take no notice unless you are irritated or angry / believes people are selfish, self-centred and unhelpful / believes people are hostile and constantly trying to put you down / believes if people do wrong they must be punished, you can't let people get way with things.

7 On a particular estate in a particular city there are around 600 children between the ages of five and fifteen. Only about fifty of them keep their rooms tidy enough to satisfy their parents. Most parents on this estate nag their children to keep their rooms tidier. Anne, on the other hand, completely 'loses her cool' with her twelve-year-old daughter.

This is because Anne believes that **things should be just how she wants them** / **believes people take no notice unless you are irritated or angry** / believes people are selfish, self-centred and unhelpful / believes people are hostile and constantly trying to put you down / **believes if people do wrong they must be punished, you can't let people get way with things**.

8 Paul feels terrible because he hit his twelve year-old son across the face because the boy hadn't done his homework and had lied to him about it.

However, Paul was prone to react this way because deep down he believes that things should be just how he wants them / **believes people take no notice unless you are irritated or angry** / believes people are selfish, self-centred and unhelpful / believes people are hostile and constantly trying to put you down / **believes if people do wrong they must be punished, you can't let people get way with things**.

9 Another driver cut across Chris' path as he was going round a roundabout. He got so angry that he 'tailgated' the other driver for five miles. Eventually, the other driver got out and confronted Chris, and there was a fight during which Chris came off very much second best.

Chris would never have behaved this way in the first place had he not believed that things should be just how he wants them / believed people take no notice unless you are irritated or angry / believed people are selfish, self-centred and unhelpful / **believed people are hostile and constantly trying to put you down / believed if people do wrong they must be punished, you can't let people get way with things**.

And you can see the terrific pay-off that each of these people would receive if only they could alter their beliefs. For example:

1 Not only would Steve not be angry when somebody leaves the bar door open, he would not get so angry when somebody got served ahead of him in the queue, when Ben doesn't buy a round of drinks when it's his turn, etc. (Importantly, this is not to say that Steve will not rectify these things, just that he won't get angry about it.)

2 Sue will not only remain calm when her son drops a mug on the floor, she would also remain calm when he forgot to take an essential item to school. (Again, this is not to say that she would not try and develop his taking more care over things.)

3 If Nigel could change his beliefs he would feel much easier about his wife contradicting him in public because he wouldn't anticipate a critical reaction from other people.

Equally, he would feel much more relaxed in a whole host of social situations for exactly the same reason.

4 If Alan, the electrician, could alter his belief that other people are always likely to be trying to take advantage of him, then he would feel less put upon when his boss asked him to do extra jobs. Equally, he would feel more relaxed in other situations too.

5 If Graham could realize that other people (including his wife Fiona, and the men she flirts with) are not always trying to put you down, he would feel much more relaxed about her playfulness. Equally, he would feel much more relaxed in a whole host of other situations.

6 The same applies to Brian. His belief that other people are hostile and likely to be putting you down resulted in very serious consequences for him when he put a broken beer mug in the face of the person who jogged his elbow. Not only could those consequences have been avoided but, had he realized that most people are not hostile in this way, he would have lived a much more relaxed and enjoyable life.

7 Anne got extremely angry with her twelve-year-old daughter because she didn't tidy her room, and Anne believes that things have got to be the way she wants, and that people take no notice unless you get angry with them. She too would be leading a much more enjoyable life if she could accept that, by and large, things tend not to be quite

how you would like them to be, but this *doesn't really matter*. And anyway, people are better 'developed' by constructive interactions rather than by getting angry with them.

8 A similar kind of thing applies to Paul, who hit his twevle-year-old son across the face. If Paul could get to realize that it's not the end of the world if things aren't just how he wants them to be and that's it's probably not true that people take no notice unless you get really angry with them, he wouldn't have done this. Equally, he stands to benefit in all sorts of situations if he can remedy those beliefs.

9 Things worked out very badly for Chris after somebody cut across his path on a roundabout and he eventually came to grief in a fight with the other driver. If only he hadn't believed that people must be punished if they do something wrong he could have avoided this. But again, this is only one example of Chris constantly giving himself a bad time because he believed that. Equally, he stands to benefit in all sorts of situations if he can remedy those beliefs.

Developing more helpful beliefs

For this we use the AA method – which, in this case, has nothing to do with too much alcohol consumption. Here it stands simply for (a) developing better Alternative beliefs and (b) Acting them out.

Here are some suggestions:

- Less helpful belief: Things should be just exactly how I want them to be. It is awful if they are not.
- Suggestion for more helpful alternative: It's nice if things are just the way I want them, but it's not the end of the world if they're not.
- Less helpful belief: People don't take any notice of you unless you show that you are irritated or angry. It is the only way of making your point.
- Suggestion for more helpful alternative: Although you can sometimes get people to do what you want by being irritable and angry with them, you never really get them on your side. So it's better to talk and persuade. Even then people won't always do what we want, but that's not the end of the world either.
- Less helpful belief: Other people are basically selfish, self-centred and unhelpful. If you want them to help you, you have to *make* them.
- Suggestion for more helpful alternative: Although there are some people who are very selfish indeed, most people will help each other out if asked.
- Less helpful belief: Other people are basically hostile. You have to be on the alert otherwise they will take any opportunity to put you down.
- Suggestion for more helpful alternative: Although there are a few people who can be quite hostile, most people basically support each other and take a good view of each other.
- Less helpful belief: If people do wrong they must be punished, you can't let people get way with things.

- Suggestion for more helpful alternative: It's better to persuade than punish, to look to the future rather than the past. Sometimes you can't even persuade and people do get away with things. So, I'll just keep up my own standards.
- Less helpful belief: It's okay to get angry with/hit policemen, bouncers, etc.
- Suggestion for more helpful alternative: Policemen, bouncers etc. are actually real people just like anybody else. It's no more reasonable to hit them than to hit any other person.
- Less helpful belief: A father/mother/foreman/manager/supervisor is *meant* to be snappy, irritable and harsh. (Where you are a father/mother/foreman/manager/ supervisor.)
- Suggestion for more helpful alternative: A father/mother/foreman/manager/ supervisor needs to set a good example. That means being friendly and supportive rather than irritable and angry.
- Less helpful belief: My father/mother/partner/son/daughter is a complete pain in the neck, it irritates me just to look at him/her. (Where there is one particular person who produces that emotional reaction in you.)
- Suggestion for more helpful alternative: My father/mother/partner/son/daughter is just like anybody else – they've got their good points and bad points. It's no use getting hung up on their bad points.

Use cue-cards if you want

Some people actually write out a small card for themselves (known as a cue-card). This has the unhelpful belief written on the one side and a more helpful alternative on the other. Sometimes people will make quite elaborate versions of these. For example, you might write the unhelpful version in red (for danger) and the more helpful version on the other side in green (for 'go'). And you might perhaps add an exhortation after the helpful version, like 'Now do it!' Some people even go off to their local print shop and get the card nicely laminated once they have got it just how they want! Whether you like your card basic or exotic, it's quite a nice idea to carry it around with you as a constant reminder. You probably won't need seven cards – it's unlikely that you are falling prey to all seven of the unhelpful beliefs, probably just one or two – in which case you just need one or two cards.

Acting it out

You will probably remember that we noted in the previous chapter that *thinking* differently is not enough. You also need to *act* on your new thoughts. New thoughts and new behavior make a terrifically powerful combination. Rather in the way that two bicycles can lean against each other and prop each other up in a perfectly stable way for ever, your new thinking is supported by your new behavior and, equally, your new behavior is supported by your new thinking. The two will constantly reinforce each other. It's the closest we are ever going to get to perpetual motion.

So how do we act it out? There are a couple of possibilities:

- Simply imagine how a person with the new, more helpful alternative belief would act and mimic that.
- Find yourself a role-model. In other words, think of somebody who acts like they believe the new improved belief, imagine what they would do, and do it.

In either case you have to do it with a degree of conviction. For example, Sue of the mug-dropping teenage son needs to really work on her belief that he is basically okay (rather than fundamentally selfish), and she would do well to set an example of friendliness and helpfulness (rather than being like a stroppy foreman) and really act like she *believes* these two new beliefs. So, rather than uttering the words 'Get a brush and sweep it up' through clenched teeth (which, admittedly would be an improvement over her previous behavior), she goes the whole hog and says 'Get a brush and sweep it up, there's a good boy,' complete with matching encouraging tone. The point is that what she is aiming for is not simply to tidy up her behavior so that it's not so wearing for her and everybody else, but to have her new, more helpful behavior in line with new, more helpful underlying beliefs, so that she is genuinely at peace with herself and other people can see that. This is clearly much better for all concerned than simply 'keeping the lid on it'.

In just the same way Steve, sitting near the door of the bar, will now realize that the five individuals who left the door open are not selfish scoundrels who deserve punishment, but perfectly okay individuals who just need to be reminded to shut the door. The way he asks them to do that will therefore be friendly and calm, in line with that belief.

Likewise, Nigel, whose wife contradicts him in public, will realize that although others might laugh when this happens, this does not indicate that they are fundamentally hostile to him, because people are mostly supportive and friendly. Acting it out, he can now join in the laughter.

Similarly Alan need not get himself into a stew by distressing himself over things not being just as he would like them to be. He can simply get on and do the job the boss asks, or not. What was winding him up was how awful it was that things were not as he would wish. Now he's resigned to that fact he can simply get on with things.

Fiona's flirting need not irritate Graham now that he accepts that neither Fiona nor other people are basically hostile, but rather that most people are friendly and supportive; he can take Fiona's behavior for the harmless amusement it is, and act things out by just joining in the fun.

Brian, too, had he accepted that most people are okay rather than hostile, would not have jumped to the conclusion that his elbow was jogged deliberately at the bar. He would have assumed it was an accident, possibly made a joke out of it, and might even have got himself a free pint.

Anne would not have lost her rag with her daughter, sitting in the bath not tidying her room. Rather than being so uptight because things were not as she would wish (the room was still untidy) and determined that the girl must be punished for her misdemeanour, she could have accepted that sometimes children have untidy rooms and that anyway her best option is to be setting a good example as a parent.

Nor need Chris have gone chasing the man who cut across his path on the roundabout. If only he had accepted that people do not need to be punished for their misde- meanours, and that sometimes they even get away with them, he could have simply acted this belief it out by keeping up his own standards and driving his car as he thinks cars should be driven – and saved himself a lot of trouble.

A role-model can be helpful

We can see from these examples that it is straightforward enough to decide on a new belief and act it out in daily life. Plenty of people do that with a lot of success and a lot of pleasure. (It is very satisfying to see yourself take charge of your own destiny, decide on sensible beliefs and act in line with them.) Other people get to exactly the same desti- nation by a different route. They think of a particular person who seems to believe the kind of beliefs we have spoken about and ask themselves, 'What would s/he do in this situation?'

For some people, imagining it makes it a lot easier to mimic it. And mimicking the behavior effectively consoli- dates the new beliefs.

The role-model can be somebody you know, like a friend or relative, or it can be somebody you've never actually met – someone you've seen on television, perhaps. One important point if you use the latter: it doesn't particularly matter if the person is like their screen persona or not. For example, my two favourite role-models are the television business troubleshooter John Harvey-Jones and ace cricket commentator Brian Johnston. Now, I've never met either of these good people, and for all I know they might have been quite different in private life from their genial demeanour on television and radio. As a matter of fact, both gentlemen are, or were – Brian Johnston sadly died a few years back – by all accounts much the same in private life as they appeared in the public eye. But my point here is that it doesn't matter; for the purpose of a role-model, it is the persona you recognize that is important.

Nor do your role-models have to match you in age or gender, or anything else. All that is important is that you can ask yourself: 'What perspective would s/he have taken on this?' and 'How would s/he have behaved in this situation?' and so on. The fact that I never quite live up to either of my models doesn't matter either; they certainly have a good effect. The key thing is that if you find yourself a good role-model s/he can lead you into behaving just how you would wish to.

Reviewing and recording

Just as in the previous chapter, reviewing and recording are great habits to get into in entrenching your new and more helpful beliefs.

'Reviewing' is literally looking again at the situation that has just passed and replaying it. You may be in the happy situation where you can enjoy reviewing how well you behaved, how well you brought into play your new beliefs and meshed them with splendid new behavior. In which case, terrific: enjoy every moment of it. And it's not just enjoyment, either; it is, as we said before, a very useful activity to review things that have gone right. When things go well you have a good template for future success, so it is useful to consolidate and examine that template. If you've handled a difficult situation well, with no irritability and anger, then go back over it, review it, enjoy the moment.

Equally, if you've handled a situation badly in your view, if you've given in to some unhelpful beliefs and matched them with irritable and angry behavior, then simply replay the situation how you think it should have gone. Remember to think the more helpful beliefs, and envisage the more helpful behavior. *That replaying of the situation the way you would have preferred it to have gone is an extremely good thing to do*; it makes it more likely that it will go that way next time. (But beware: it is rather unhelpful simply to replay your *wrong* handling of the situation. It's best to regard that as 'water under the bridge'.)

SUMMARY

- In this chapter we have covered how our beliefs affect the way we appraise and judge a situation, and as a consequence how we behave in that situation.

- We have listed the most common unhelpful beliefs that affect people's perceptions of the situations in which they find themselves.
- We have listed the more helpful alternative beliefs to replace the unhelpful ones.
- We have looked at the method for replacing unhelpful beliefs with helpful ones. This involves the AA method: highlighting the Alternative helpful belief and Acting out the situation in line with those beliefs.
- We have looked at the importance of reviewing successes and consolidating them as templates for good future behavior, and also of reviewing failures – but reminding ourselves how we would have preferred to act in the situation, so we are more likely to get it right next time!

PROJECT

- Get yourself a piece of paper and write down any of the unhelpful beliefs that you think apply to you.
- For each of them, write down the more helpful belief. This might be a question of simply copying down what I've written above, or you might want to put it into your own words.
- Replay a recent situation where your unhelpful beliefs have led you to appraise a situation badly and react in an irritable and angry way. Replay how you would have seen the situation if you had had your more helpful beliefs in place, and what you would have done. (For example, if you are Steve you would replay sitting at the bar by the door, now believing that people, even those who leave doors open, are basically okay, appraising the situation differently and asking, in a proper friendly way, each person to close the door). Make it a good vivid replay in your mind.

- Most important of all, practise your new beliefs, seeing every situation through the eyes of someone who has these new beliefs, or through the eyes of a role-model you've settled on. Then match your behavior to your new perceptions – just as Steve would do in the previous point.
- Each time you have success, review that success and enjoy the moment. Review how your new beliefs helped, and how your new behavior was in line with those beliefs. If you 'let yourself down', review the incident *the way you would have preferred it to have gone*. Pretty soon you will have lots of 'good' reviews and not many of the other sort!

12

Cats, camels and recreation: Anger

Daft title for a chapter. Never mind, you might as well read it because it could just be very relevant to yourself. For some people it will be spot-on.

Remember the model we're working on as trigger, appraisal/judgement, anger, inhibitions, response (see Figure 12.1).What we are talking about in this chapter is the 'anger' box; and there are just three points to make about it.

Displacing anger

The first point is that *anger can be displaced*. This process is commonly known as 'kicking the cat' or 'always hurting the one you love'. For example, you may have a bad day at work, but judge that it is a bad career move to get angry with your boss. What you do, therefore, is to come home and (metaphorically, of course!) kick the cat: in other words, take it out on whoever or whatever happens to be around.

The strange thing is that whoever or whatever turns out to be on the receiving end of your anger does in fact seem to be very irritating at the time in question. You are not always aware that you are 'displacing' your anger from your boss at work on to your loved ones/cat at home.

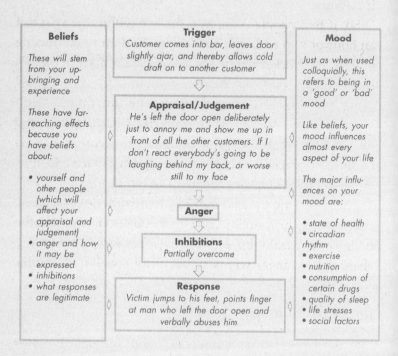

Figure 12.1 A model for analyzing irritability and anger

Anger is additive

The second point is that *anger is additive*: it builds up. Again, the best analogy is the leaky bucket that we first used in Part One. Suppose you have a bucket with holes in it; it is still possible to fill the bucket to overflowing by pouring in several jugs of water in quick succession. When the bucket overflows, that's the equivalent of an outburst of anger or irritability.

So, if five people come into the bar within the space of an hour or two and each one leaves the door open causing a draft, the bucket overflows (or at least it does in Steve's case) and an outburst occurs. If those same five people came into the bar over a six-month period, and on each occasion Steve was sitting near the door, it is unlikely that he would have an outburst on the fifth occasion. This is because his anger would have been given a chance to 'leak away' on each occasion before the next 'top-up'.

This 'building up' is commonly known as the 'last straw that breaks the camel's back' phenomenon. I prefer the image of the leaky bucket, however, because, given half a chance, your anger will normally 'leak away' quite nicely.

Recreational anger

The third point to be made here, and perhaps the most important one, concerns what I call 'recreational anger'. Let me give you an example. Please don't be put off by the fact that this is a very extreme example; the same phenomenon happens day in, day out.

Very early on in my career, when I was working as a prison psychologist, I came across a prisoner who was having quite a lot of trouble serving his sentence; he got tense and agitated, and periodically smashed up his cell. I taught him how to relax and did some general 'counselling' work with him, with the result that he confided in me that he had been beaten up by half a dozen prison officers in the previous prison he had been held in. (I have no idea how true this allegation was, but that was what he told me.)

Anyway, he'd formed a plan that, on release, he would go and track down these six prison officers, and one by one shoot them.

I took this very seriously, (a) because I was young and naïve and took everything seriously, and (b) because he was already in prison for having shot somebody, so clearly he had the wherewithal to do what he said he was going to do. Furthermore he described how, on his previous sentence, he had done exactly the same thing: that is, he had spent time thinking and planning about how, when he got out, he would shoot this person. And, sure enough, he had done exactly that, and here he was back in prison again for that crime.

Now, it would be nice to think that young prison psychologists know exactly what to do in such a situation, but I have to tell you that I didn't. So we simply got to talking around it, him telling me all about how it was . . .

To cut a long story short, he was in the habit of whiling away hour after hour fantasizing about how he was going to get his revenge. This, apparently, was entirely pleasurable, and time flew by while he did this.

And this was the first case I came across of 'recreational anger': anger which at the very least passes the time of day, sometimes actually gives you a 'buzz' and often puts you into a different state of mind, so that actions which wouldn't normally seem sensible and rational options look like just that. Going back to our leaky bucket analogy, it is as though you've plugged up all the holes in the bucket, keen to hang on to all the water there, and then just spend the time looking at the water. Or, rather more literally, you do everything to prevent your anger from drifting away and spend time mulling it over.

The best course of action to take in this situation is as follows:

- Don't do whatever your anger is telling you to do.
- Do something else.

Let's expand on that a little. When you are very irritable and angry it is as though that anger takes you over. The anger actually tells you to do things that, in your normal state, you wouldn't do. So who are you going to take more notice of, your anger or you yourself?

Well, the answer is obvious: it's more important to be true to yourself than to some temporary state of anger. On the other hand, it is very difficult simply to *refrain* from doing something. Rather like 'not thinking of a giraffe', it is virtually impossible. If someone tells you *not* to think of a giraffe, a picture of a long dappled neck springs into mind no matter how carefully you try to obey. In the same way, not to do what your anger tells you is very tricky indeed.

Getting away from anger

The answer is to *concentrate on doing something else*. Anything. Real-life examples of alternatives that people turn to in this situation include the following:

- Take physical exercise: walk, run, swim, etc.
- Read a book, magazine, newspaper.
- Watch television or listen to the radio.
- Go and do some gardening.
- Phone up or go and see a friend.
- Simply take yourself out of the situation and go somewhere else.

All of these are equivalent to 'doing something else'. And that is sufficient for most of us. In the case of the prisoner I was just telling you about, tactics such as reading a book would not be sufficient, because he had a long-term problem, ten times the size of anything afflicting most of us. Nevertheless, with him, we adopted exactly the same strategy, and he did indeed 'do something else'. He got in touch with a woman who ran a hostel for ex-prisoners and wrote to her to see whether that was somewhere he could stay after release. Thank goodness, she wrote back telling him that might well be an option and, most importantly, including a photograph of the actual hostel. I am sure that it was that photograph that really swung it for him. Now he could literally envisage what else he could do upon leaving prison. Rather than going up to his previous prison and slowly stalking the six prison officers concerned, he could catch a train to this hostel and settle there. Happily, it was in a totally different part of the country.

Well, all that sounds very sensible, doesn't it? So why don't people do it? When you feel really angry and your anger is telling you to do something drastic, why do you tend to do it even though the rational part of you knows that this is a temporary state you're in?

I think one of the reasons is that some people think it is more 'honest' to give vent to their anger. Personally, I wouldn't go along with that. 'Honesty' is a splendid characteristic when it means (a) not lying or (b) not stealing from other people, but a very destructive characteristic when it is used to mean (c) saying very tactless and hurtful things on the grounds that 'I'm only being honest' or (d) simply giving vent to angry urges without any thought of the consequences for yourself or other people.

Give yourself time

There's one important reason why it is always sensible, first, to refrain from doing what your anger is telling you, and second, to do something else. This is because, once you have truly regained your emotional equilibrium, you can decide at leisure what you think is best to do about the situation, rather than letting your anger tell you.

Let me give you an example. Graham described to me how on one occasion he was so agitated by his wife Fiona's flirting that, even while still at the party they were both attending, he was going through in his mind how he was going to leave Fiona and, more particularly, how he was going to tell Fiona about his decision. He was relishing, in a strange sort of way, how this would 'teach her a lesson' and how sorry she would be.

And it was more by luck than judgement that this did not come to pass. In the car going home he was 'sulking' but in fact still rehearsing what he was going to say and still enjoying the anticipated effect. At home, the sulk continued but, as I say, more by luck than judgement he decided to postpone the confrontation until the next morning and simply go to sleep for the time being. Happily, by the next morning sleep had worked its magic, anger had retreated to a back seat and, although the discussion was rather heated, it was not so vitriolic as it would have been the previous evening. So, by accident, Graham had followed the formula: Don't do what your anger tells you, do something else (in this case, go to sleep).

Graham is one of my favourite cases, for two reasons. First, there are lots of Grahams who have not worked things out so well for themselves: in other words, men who have allowed their anger to tell them what to do and whose marriages have disintegrated as a result. Second, in Graham's case, he was able eventually to do a complete review of his judgements and beliefs, rather along the lines of that set out in the previous two chapters, and ended up seeing things in a completely different light. The net result was that Fiona's flirting did not simply become 'not irritating', it became a positive asset to their relationship once he realized that it was perfectly harmless, and, perhaps more to the point, that everybody else knew that it had no serious intent.

SUMMARY

- In talking about anger there are three points to be made. First, it can be displaced so that, although it might be your boss who has caused your anger, your partner or somebody else actually receives it. Second, anger is *additive* by nature. Envisage your anger as water in a leaky bucket. If another jug full of anger arrives before the first jug-full has been allowed to leak away, then your bucket is filling up. Eventually, if a third, fourth or fifth jug-full arrives, the bucket might overflow, leading to an angry outburst. Third, there is such a thing as 'recreational anger', where you get a peculiar kind of buzz from simply dwelling upon your anger and what you're going to do about it.

- Probably the best analogy for anger is the 'leaky bucket'. If it is topped up too quickly, then yes, it can overflow; but given half a chance, anger will leak away over a period of time.

- No matter whether your anger is about to overflow, or whether you're in a state of recreational anger, or anything else, the best policy is (a) don't allow your anger to tell you what to do and (b) do *any*thing else. Only when you've gained a good sense of equilibrium should you decide what to do about the situation that prompted the anger.

- The use of a role-model (a person you use as a good example), as discussed in Chapter 11, can be very powerful here. You can simply ask yourself 'What would X [your model] do right now?' Interestingly, your anger will fight back and tell you to get on with allowing it to have its head. Just put it on hold for a moment, and really get to imagining what your good role-model would do in the given situation.

PROJECT

- One of the most important lessons in this chapter has been how to differentiate between what your anger tells you to do and what you yourself want to do. Therefore a very relevant project is to work on becoming more aware of both of these 'voices'. What I mean is, next time you are feeling angry, work out (a) what your anger is telling you to do and (b) what your 'real self' would tell you to do.

- It's good to practise this in situations which make you only *slightly* angry. The reason for this is that when you are *very* angry the 'angry voice' shouts so loud that it drowns out your 'true self' voice. You therefore have to practise being attuned to your 'true self' voice in mild-anger situations so that, eventually, you can hear it even in high-anger situations.

- And remember, most of us want to be loyal to our true self rather than to what anger tells us to do.

13

Putting the brakes on: Inhibitions

As we have said before, some people view inhibitions as bad things to have. They think in terms of 'being inhibited', equating it with being shy, withdrawn and a shade socially inadequate.

In our context the reverse is the case. Remember where the inhibitions box fits into our model (Figure 13.1).

The point here is that anger is an emotion which we may or may not choose to make other people aware of. So it is perfectly possible for somebody to be angry with you without you realizing it, simply because they choose not to tell you or not to demonstrate it in any way. And, of course the reverse holds true as well: it is perfectly possible for you to be feeling very irritable and angry and for other people to be totally unaware of it. This rather useful phenomenon is all thanks to our inhibitions. It is no accident that there is an area of the brain whose specific function is to inhibit the expression of every emotion that might occur.

This area of the brain can be damaged temporarily, for example by alcohol, or permanently by injury or some illnesses. Happily, however, it can also be developed. In this chapter we will look at inhibitions, why we want to use them, and how we can develop our ability to use them.

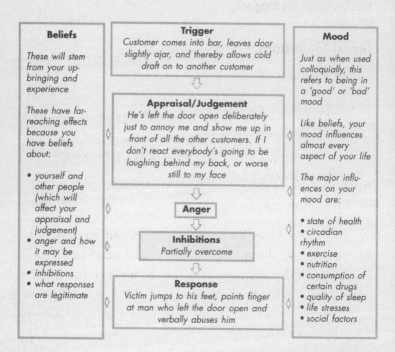

Figure 13.1 A model for analyzing irritability and anger

Internal and external inhibitions

Inhibitions fall into two categories:

- moral, or 'internal' inhibitions;
- practical, or 'external' inhibitions.

Leaving aside how we bring these inhibitions to mind at the crucial time just for the moment, let's have a look at each of these categories.

Moral inhibitions

Some examples of moral inhibitions are

- 'It is wrong to go around snapping at people.'
- 'It is wrong to be frequently angry with people.'
- 'It is wrong to hit people.'

. . . and so on. Over thousands of years philosophers have given a lot of thought to what makes actions moral or otherwise, and various schemes have been proposed. One such is the 'What if everybody did this?' argument, and this is probably one of the more relevant ones here. If everybody goes around snapping at one another, being angry with one another, hitting one another, then clearly the world is going to be an extremely unrewarding place. Therefore, if it is not okay for everybody to do it, how can it be okay for you to do it?

Another basis for morality is the 'adhering to set rules' scheme, of which the Ten Commandments is one example. And this is indeed a powerful constraint on people's behavior. We all set ourselves rules which control our behavior – down to the finest detail, sometimes. Some of these rules can be very strange and even abhorrent. For example, there are men who hold to the rule that 'You never hit a woman, unless you're living with her.' Now what possible ethical basis can such a rule have? None that I or the majority of people can see; but even so, this rule governs the behavior of some men.

Some rules are imposed on us by society and most of us sign up to them. Examples include 'You don't stab people,' 'You don't shoot people,' and 'You don't hit people.' But of course, not everybody signs up to all of these rules. Most people sign up to the first two of those three, but a significant number do not sign up to the third. I say that simply because many parents hit their children, although they usually use a euphemism such as 'slap' or 'smack' or 'spank'.

Once you start setting rules for yourself, over and above those that society imposes, then things can get surprisingly complicated, especially in view of the fact that this should be a fairly simple business. For example, before our children were born, my wife and I set a rule for ourselves that we would never hit them. A good rule, we thought, and indeed we have abided by it. But even this has major snags, which I will tell you about.

Just before I do, though, I would like to you to contemplate an incident I witnessed walking through the pedestrian area of a city centre. Nearby, a woman was walking along with her two children of perhaps eight and ten. As they walked along, she was hitting one of them backwards and forwards across the head, saying to him as she did so: 'How many times have I told you not to hit your brother?'

The contradictory nature of the mother's words and behavior somehow produced an almost humorous side to this sorry sight. Nevertheless, the 'Give him a taste of his own medicine' thinking that she was demonstrating is common enough. Sadly, however, the all-powerful effect of modelling will probably overwhelm everything else. The young lad will be left with the simple observation that 'It is okay to hit people, even my mother does it.'

But back to my own dilemmas. There we were, smugly bringing up our kids without hitting/smacking/slapping them. And did this mean that they behaved like angels? No, of course it didn't; in fact they behaved just like all other kids. For example, when young, they would shout, squabble, pinch and hit each other. Shout, in particular. So how did I resolve the situation, how did I intervene to stop them shouting and quarrelling? Well, naturally, I shouted louder than either of them.

This usually worked in the short term, but was it a good policy? Clearly not, because I was simply doing exactly the same as I had seen the woman in the pedestrian area doing: trying to quell a behavior by exhibiting exactly the same behavior. So what lesson would my children learn? Presumably 'It's okay to shout, even my father does it.'

'Modelling' is the key concept here. This simply refers to the 'model' or 'example' you set. And in the case of parents and children, the example set is a very powerful one.

Here's another instance of the power of rule-setting. Richard was a young man who had come to see me because he had taken to terminating arguments with his girlfriend by hitting her. The sequence of events seemed to be that they would start arguing, both would start shouting at each other, and the process would only come to an end when he hit her. He then felt terribly guilty, she felt terrible, and this was putting an understandable strain on the whole relationship. And yet, he seemed unable to stop. This was surely strange; one might say, 'If he doesn't want to do it, why doesn't he *stop* doing it?' But, as so often is the case, he seemed to be the victim of his own behavior. Richard was unable to help himself and so turned to outside help through therapy.

Richard and I talked about his background and he told me about his school and college days (which weren't long ago; he was only in his early twenties at the time). In particular he told me how he seemed to be a natural target for bullying. Even in his last year at school a particular fellow student used to pick on him. On one occasion this youth picked on him once too often and, probably accidentally, ripped his shirt. Richard told me how, when this happened, something snapped inside him. Apparently uncontrollably, he just grabbed hold of his tormentor and gave him a thorough pummelling. Unsurprisingly, perhaps, this put an end to the whole sad sequence of events. Not only did the tormentor stop tormenting Richard, he also seemed to be genuinely remorseful.

Equally unsurprisingly, Richard felt rather pleased with himself; it seemed that he had discovered the answer to many of life's problems, although in fairness he did not phrase it consciously and openly to himself in this way. Nevertheless, it was about six months after that incident that he first hit his girlfriend. And from then on there was no turning back; the pattern was established.

So the question is: What rule had Richard established for himself? It seemed to be something like: 'It's okay to hit people, in fact it will solve a lot of problems.'

And yet, when we examine the evidence, this only seemed to be partially true. In the one instance, leaving aside as to whether Richard was 'right' to hit the other guy, it had worked well for him. With his girlfriend, it was working very badly for both of them.

I asked him to try out a new rule, namely: 'It's sometimes okay to get into fights with males my own age, but no one else.' He tried it out, experimentally at first; then, gradually, he 'bought into' the rule and really adopted it as his own. On his subsequent appointments he came with his girlfriend, and they told me this new approach was working very well for them. (Incidentally, happily Richard did *not* then go around getting into fights with males his own age. In fact, he seemed to be naturally a very peaceable kind of character.)

So, we have a first category of inhibitions, the moral category. These inhibitions may be established by the question 'What if everybody went around doing this?' This principle will tend to preclude us from indiscriminately snapping, shouting, hitting. The other yardstick for these moral inhibitions is 'obedience to a rule'. Many rules are the laws of the land and it's obviously best to go by those. Others, like not hitting children, we make up for ourselves. Even so, they are very powerful determinants of our behavior. I mentioned in an earlier chapter the man at the bar who stopped himself being hit by saying to his would-be assailant, 'Hey, I'm over forty.' By the time the would-be assailant checked through his list of rules to see whether there was one which said 'You don't hit men over forty' the moment had passed.

Practical inhibitions

The second category of inhibitions is practical; nothing to do with morality. Inhibitions in this category limit our behavior by reminding us of the dire consequences that might befall us if we don't observe them.

Exercise

Below, I have listed some of the examples we have talked about in this book, in the form of questions which invite you to say why the person in question doesn't just do the very thing that occurs to them. I have filled the first three in to show you the kind of thing that's in my mind.

1   Gerry is intensely irritated by his noisy neighbours playing their music over-loud next-door to him. What practical considerations stop him going around and giving his neighbours a real piece of his mind?

    Answer: He believes that if he did that, they would probably play their music even louder. And in any case, the guy next door is bigger than Gerry so he feels he must treat him with some respect.

2   Colin is intensely irritated by his neighbours' kids playing football in the street outside and allowing

their ball to run all over his garden. What stops him going around and giving the kids and their parents a good piece of his mind?

Answer: See above. In this case, too, Colin thinks the kids will probably just behave worse, and laugh and jeer at him every time they see him, and the parents might indeed encourage them to do that.

3 Pam is intensely irritated by the noise that her husband makes when he is eating. What stops her from jumping up, banging the table and shouting: 'For God's sake why can't you eat like a normal human being?'

Answer: She's afraid that if she did that it would bring to a head the whole disharmony in the marriage. He would realize that her irritation was not really with his eating, but with him in general; and that his noisy eating symbolizes something deeper, to her.

4 When a fifth man comes into a bar and leaves the door open, Steve is so angry that, when he gets up, he would like to punch the man straight in the face. What stops him doing this?

5 Judy takes her small daughter to the outpatient department and has to wait two hours before they are seen by the doctor and nurse. While she is waiting she finds that all the patients there (at least twenty of them) have been given the same (2 p.m.) appointment. What she would like to do is to really let rip at the doctor and nurse, who, by the way, were busy drinking tea together and not seeing their patients for at least a quarter of an hour. What stops her doing this?

6 Nigel is frequently irritated by his wife contradicting him while they are out in public. What he would like to do when, for example, she corrects him that the event he is humorously describing didn't take place on a Wednesday, as he says, but on a Tuesday, is, there and then, to give her a real piece of his mind, and shout at her: 'What the hell difference does it make whether it was a Wednesday or a Tuesday?' What prevents him from doing this?

7 Alan is frequently asked by his boss to do more
   work than he thinks he should be asked to. He would
   like to tell him where to get off, but doesn't, he
   simply goes home irritable. What stops Alan giving
   his boss a mouthful?

   _____

   _____

   _____

   _____

8 Chris, who drives a smart four-wheel drive, is annoyed
   by the bad driving of a character in an old wreck.
   Chris chases after him and, when the other car has to
   pause at the next roundabout, feels like driving straight
   up the back of him. What stops him doing this?

   _____

   _____

   _____

   _____

9 Ken is an executive who is so stressed out that when
   a customer asks him to do one more thing (which
   in fact is good business) he feels like telling him to
   get lost, or words to that effect. What prevents him
   from doing this?

   _____

   _____

   _____

   _____

10 Bob has not got much time for the police so, when he is stopped late one night and asked where he is going and what he is doing, he feels like telling the police officer to mind his own business. In truth, he feels like thumping him. What stops Bob from doing this?

_____

_____

_____

_____

11 Tina has a thing about 'bouncers' at the entrance to clubs. So, when a bouncer stops her and her friend from going into a particular club, she screams and shouts at him and launches an apparently energetic attack – but one which, in reality, has no force in it. Why does she not launch a proper full-blooded attack on the bouncer?

_____

_____

_____

_____

Below are what seem to be the answers from the people in question. See how they match up with what you wrote.

4 When a fifth man comes into a bar and leaves the door open, Steve is so angry that, when he gets up,

he would like to punch the man straight in the face. What stops him doing this?

Answer: He knows he would get banned from the bar, and his friends Ben and Chris probably wouldn't speak to him again either.

5 Judy takes her small daughter to the outpatient department and has to wait two hours before they are seen by the doctor and nurse. While she is waiting she finds that all the patients there (at least twenty of them) have been given the same (2 p.m.) appointment. What she would like to do is to really let rip at the doctor and nurse, who, by the way, were busy drinking tea together and not seeing their patients for at least a quarter of an hour. What stops her doing this?

Answer: Judy's main concern is to get the best possible treatment for her daughter. She doesn't want the doctor to be distracted by anything else, nor does she want him to 'take it out on them'.

6 Nigel is frequently irritated by his wife contradicting him while they are out in public. What he would like to do when, for example, she corrects him that the event he is humorously describing didn't take place on a Wednesday, as he says, but on a Tuesday, is, there and then, to give her a real piece of his mind, and shout at her: 'What the hell difference does it make whether it was a Wednesday or a Tuesday?' What prevents him from doing this?

Answer: The knowledge that that would be the end of the evening as far as everyone is concerned. In other words, a ghastly uneasy silence would descend upon everybody until someone made some feeble joke to try to break it.

7 Alan is frequently asked by his boss to do more work than he thinks he should be asked to. He would like to tell him where to get off, but doesn't, he simply goes home irritable. What stops Alan giving his boss a mouthful?

Answer: Alan is afraid that, after a few occasions like that, he might be heading for the sack, or, at best, pretty limited career prospects.

8 Chris, who drives a smart four-wheel drive, is annoyed by the bad driving of a character in an old wreck. Chris chases after him and, when the other car has to pause at the next roundabout, feels like driving straight up the back of him. What stops him doing this?

Answer: He knows that will probably cause a serious accident as a result of which he, Chris, will find himself in court; and the very least that will happen is that he will be banned from driving.

9 Ken is an executive who is so stressed out that when a customer asks him to do one more thing (which in fact is good business) he feels like telling him to get lost, or words to that effect. What prevents him from doing this?

Answer: He knows he would lose that customer, who would then go around bad-mouthing the firm, and gradually the firm would shrink and disappear.

10 Bob has not got much time for the police so, when he is stopped late one night and asked where he is going and what he is doing, he feels like telling the police officer to mind his own business. In truth, he feels like thumping him. What stops Bob from doing this?

Answer: He knows he'll probably end up being arrested and charged, and will lose out in some major way.

11 Tina has a thing about 'bouncers' at the entrance to clubs. So, when a bouncer stops her and her friend from going into a particular club, she screams and shouts at him and launches an apparently energetic attack – but one which, in reality, has no force in it. Why does she not launch a proper full-blooded attack on the bouncer?

Answer: She knows she would come off second best, and anyway doesn't want to do anything that could be seen as 'an assault'.

It's clear that these inhibitions have nothing at all to do with 'morality'. They are entirely to do with practical consequences and not wanting to lose out in some way. Entirely sensible, in fact.

So why do we get irritable and what do we do about it?

A perfectly reasonable question is: 'If there are so many moral and practical reasons for us to inhibit our irritability and anger, why do we ever feel that way? Humans aren't normally designed to feel and do things that have no purpose, so what's the purpose in this case?'

The main answer seems to be that it is a feedback mechanism – a way of letting other people know that what they are doing is going down badly with you. A way, therefore, of people becoming socialized and working together as a society rather than a collection of competing individuals.

In that case, why should we inhibit our inhibition and anger? If it fulfils this useful function of informing people when we feel they are they are 'out of order', presumably if we inhibit it then everything will go haywire. Other people will trample all over us, secure that there is no payback.

Well, if taken to extremes, that would be true. If you were never to show any irritation, never to show any anger, this would probably be confusing for people. They wouldn't know when you were pleased and when you were displeased; it would be quite disorientating for those you mixed with.

But there is a happy medium. Some people we know are decidedly 'irritable'. We are not suggesting that they should *never* show any irritation or anger; that would probably be super-human (and, as we have just noted, not very helpful). There are things in life that *are* irritating, things which prompt a 'normal' person to show some irritation. When we describe a person as 'irritable', however, s/he is going too far, becoming irritated by things that wouldn't irritate a 'normal' person, or getting more irritated than most by slightly irritating things.

So, as ever, it is not a question of 'all or nothing'. Yes, it is sometimes just as well for people to be able to sense that we are irritated or angry. On the other hand, it is very easy to take this much too far, to the point where even the slightest thing irritates us, or where we become irritated if things are not *exactly* as we want them. In that case our irritation and anger mechanism is clearly over-functioning, to the extent that it is counter-productive. When it is functioning at just the right level it provides useful feedback to other people; they can sense when we are slightly irritated and angry with what they are doing and as a result will probably desist. If it is functioning in too extreme a way, those around us get frightened and worried, and our relationships begin to break down.

A good parallel is with jealousy and possessiveness. Most people rather like their loved ones to exhibit a small amount of jealousy and possessiveness towards them. If this is not the case, many people take it as an indication that they are not really loved. So, a small amount of jealousy and possessiveness is perfectly fine, even a good thing. But what happens when this is taken too far? When someone spends all their waking moments worried about what their loved one is doing, whether they are being faithful and loyal? Some people go to the extent of popping home unexpectedly, leaving listening devices around the house or on the phone, even hiring private detectives to follow their loved ones around.

Clearly, this level of jealousy and possessiveness is counter-productive and is very quickly going to lead to a breakdown in the relationship.

So, in both instances, whether we are talking about irritability and anger or jealousy and possessiveness, you can have too much of a good thing. In fact, rather like a homoeopathic medicine, the right amount is very little indeed!

Putting the brakes on

We can see, then, that for all sorts of moral and practical reasons we want to limit our irritability and anger very severely – almost to the extent of stopping it before it gets going. If we keep it down to very low levels it can work extremely well for us and for everybody around us; if we let it get any higher the reverse is the case: it works really badly for us and all around us.

So how do we perform this difficult balancing act, of keeping any irritation and anger down to useful and beneficial levels – down to those very subtle levels where those around us actually feel pleased to see the very occasional irritation from us, simply because it gives them feedback about what is happening?

For a task as complex as this we need a simple analogy. The best I know is that of traffic lights. If you drive around any reasonably large town you will find there is a complex system of interacting traffic lights. For example, near where I live there is a ring road round which I have to drive to get to the motorway. At one point on this ring road there is a particularly distinctive sequence of lights. The first set normally brings you to a halt; for some reason they usually seem to be on red. While you sit waiting at these lights, you can also see that the second set of lights you have to go through is also on red. In due course your first set turns to green, and you move off. If you go off at a very moderate pace, by the time you reach the second set (which is only 40 or 50 metres away) those too are changing to green and you can sail across, although you do have to keep your wits thoroughly about you during this procedure. The same applies to a third set of lights, again only 40 to 50 metres ahead; these too are in sequence with the first and second sets, and you can time things to get across all three in one steady passage.

In summary, what would be a completely unruly flow of traffic is first of all brought to a halt, then allowed to proceed in a thoroughly orderly and controlled fashion. Of course, there are other roads crossing the road I am on, hence the need for lights. An aerial view of this whole procedure would reveal an amazing number of vehicles, all meshing superbly and proceeding at as reasonable a pace as they possibly can. A real feat of interaction and coordination.

Exactly the same happens when two or more people are interacting with each other. Each individual has their own senses of direction, their own pace they want to keep up, their own interests. At the same time they are very keen to mesh with one another, not only because they know that is to their mutual advantage, but also because it's enjoyable and satisfying.

So how does the traffic lights analogy work in practice?

Remarkably simply. All we have to do is learn to spot a red light! And that's easy. Any amount of irritation or anger we feel is, effectively, a red light. So we don't just barge across it; that way lies disaster.

When confronted with a red light, irritation and anger in other words, we stop. This is not a 'give way' sign; it is very definitely a 'stop' one. We really have to make sure we come to a complete halt. Sometimes people say 'count to ten'. Well, you can do this if you want; certainly it brings things to a pretty marked stop. On the other hand, you can simply note the presence of the 'red light' (irritability and anger), carry on talking about whatever you like, and then, when the irritability and anger have subsided to a tiny amount (the lights change) you can get ready to move on to say whatever you think is best.

How does that work in practice? Here are some real examples, the first of which – you will not be surprised to learn – concerns Steve, in a draft at the bar.

1 Steve at the bar

Red light: Yet another man comes in, leaving the door open. Steve experiences a sudden surge of anger, which he recognizes as a red light.

Wait: Quickly, almost instantly, Steve's anger drops to a very low level. Simply refraining from speaking for a moment has helped. He judges the best thing to say.

Green light: Steve leans over towards the man who has just come in and is about to walk past, and says: 'Push the door to, would you, friend, it leaves a heck of a draft.'

And, moreover, he can repeat this sequence time and again, just as he can manage hundreds of traffic lights on a journey.

2 Ian dropping mug on floor, irritates Sue

Red light: The sound of the mug smashing on the floor produces a sudden surge in adrenaline in Sue, which she recognizes as the red light. She says nothing for an instant, while the anger quickly drops to a more minor level.

Wait: With her anger at a much lower level, she works out the best response.

Green light: Still with a trace of irritation in her voice, she says: 'Get a brush and sweep that up and put it in the bin, there's a good boy.'

Again, this is an interesting one, because it is not just mugs that Ian breaks; in truth, he is somewhat careless. It is therefore probably appropriate that Sue's voice has just a dash of irritation in it. It's certainly very genuine, she really feels the irritation. But by thinking in terms of the traffic lights procedure she puts it into a useful context rather than a destructive one.

3 Vicky tells of Danny and her underwear

Red light: Danny felt intensely angry that Vicky had broken a very intimate confidence, not just to a few other people, but on the radio. This intense anger persisted for several days. He therefore said nothing.

Wait: When the anger subsided to a more manageable level, Danny worked out the best way to approach the subject.

Green light: At a moment when there was plenty of time, and he and Vicky were getting on reasonably well, he said: 'I'll tell you something I think we should talk about, because you know I was really angry about what you said on the radio the other day. It seems to me we should talk about what needs to be kept between the two of us and what can be said to others, because I know both of us come under pressure from smart interviewers to say things we'd rather not say. So I guess we ought to get our act together now about how we're going to cope with that.'

4 Anne finds her daughter in the bath rather than tidying her bedroom

Red light: Anne, having thought that her daughter was at last tidying her room, goes up and finds that is not the case. Gradually she realizes that, in fact, the girl is in the bath. Feeling furious, she refrains from doing anything for a little while.

Wait: Anne's initial burst of outrage has now subsided to a lower and perhaps useful level of irritation. She works out the best way to move forward.

Green light: Helen decides to wait until her daughter is out of the bath and dressed again. Then she goes to her room and says, with the tiniest hint of irritation, a large dash of determination, and also a smidgen of friendliness: 'Look, dear, we're really going to have to get this room of yours tidied. So come on, I'll help you with it.'

The traffic lights technique is a remarkably strong and powerful one. But there are several points to be made.

Sometimes the 'red light' stays on for a very short period of time, barely a second or two. Steve in the bar, and Sue with Ian who drops the mug on the floor, are examples of this. In other cases the red light stays on for hours or even days – as with Danny and Vicky.

Secondly, you don't always get what you want. Anne is an example of this. She never got to the point where her daughter set about happily tidying her bedroom all on her own. And we have to recognize that there's no law that says we should get what we want, any more than other people always get what they want. There's no need to 'awfulize' this phenomenon. It's just the way things are.

The third point, and the best news, is that just as we get good at coping with real traffic lights, we also get good at coping with these metaphorical ones. So, whereas previously Steve became more and more incensed every time somebody left the door to the bar open, he now became more and more skilled at going through the traffic lights procedure. So each time he said 'Push the door to, would you, friend, it leaves a heck of a draft,' it seemed like the first time he had said it as far as the hearer was concerned; but in fact, this was now a skilled procedure he had developed.

Likewise, and perhaps in particular, for Sue with Ian the mug-breaker. Ian gave Sue plenty of practice in spotting red lights, but Sue did her bit by recognizing them and moving through them efficiently and productively.

EXERCISE

- Think of a 'red light' that has occurred over the last two days: something that actually made you angry, or potentially could have done.
- Did you recognize it as any sort of a red light and stop at that point?
- Did you stop and wait for the anger to subside to a very small amount and then decide on your best way forward? Did you then move off along the productive path you've chosen?

Well, unless you've read this book before, presumably you've answered no to one or more of those questions. So here is another …

EXERCISE

- Again, what exactly was the 'red light'? In other words, what happened to make you angry?
- What would 'stopping' have meant in that situation? In other words, could you simply have said nothing, or would that have looked strange? Would you perhaps have had to carry on talking in some way or carry on doing what you were doing? In that case the 'red light' is simply not responding to your anger but instead carrying on with what you were doing.
- When your anger has subsided to a low level, what would have been the best path to take? This is the amber phase: your anger is at a low level, and *you* (not your anger) are deciding on the best way forward.
- What exactly would 'green' have looked like? In other words, what would you have said or done? What tone of voice would you have used?

If this all sounds very complicated, that's misleading. It is a very simple and very enjoyable procedure. It is best, however, to go through it in your mind a few times, just as the second of these two exercises suggests. Each time you hit 'red', recognize it as such, allow the anger to subside to a very low level, and then decide on your best way forward. Then move forward, actually do what you've decided on (green).

TIP

There is only one trap in this procedure, and that is to kid yourself that you're at amber when in fact you're still on red. Remember, the characteristic of being at amber is that your irritation and anger are at *very low levels*. Sometimes, it is true, this may be just half a second after the intense initial burst of anger. At other times, however, it is a good while afterwards.

SUMMARY

In this chapter we have looked at:

- The types of inhibitions that exist: *moral* inhibitions based either on 'What would happen if everybody did this?' or on 'clear rules', and *practical* inhibitions, which are based simply on the practical consideration of what would happen either for you or for other people if you acted on your raw anger.

- Why we get irritable and angry: the idea that a very low level of irritability and anger provides useful feedback to those around us, while anything above this very low level is counterproductive and simply puts everybody on edge.

- How we can bring inhibitions to mind when we want them, and act on them usefully by using the traffic lights procedure.

PROJECT

Three projects come out of this chapter:

1 Read through all the material on inhibitions and get it really clear in your mind what your inhibitions are. Remember, these inhibitions are going to prove really useful to you. They're the 'motivators' for you to keep your irritability and anger down to a very, very low level. Write them down.

2 The practical project is the traffic lights one. Really practice spotting 'red lights'. In other words, practice spotting when you become angry. Allow it to sink to a low level (amber) as quickly as possible. *Only at that point* do you decide what would be a reasonable way forward. Then, when you've decided, move on to green; in other words, put into practice what you think is the best way forward. And remember, just like Anne, you can't always have your own way!

3 As ever, review your successes, either mentally or on paper.

14

The bottom line: Response

You know what they mean by 'the bottom line'? It comes from business and refers to the bottom line of the accounts: the final profit (or loss) figure. It doesn't matter whether the head of the business has been extremely hard-working and everyone else in the firm incredibly conscientious, if the bottom line is that the business made a loss then that, in a sense, is all that matters. Conversely, it doesn't matter that another business might have a lazy and lethargic head and an opportunistic workforce; if the bottom line is that they are making a healthy profit, then that, in a sense, is all that matters.

It's the same here. In our model (Figure 14.1) we are now looking at the 'response' box. The point is that if our final response is an acceptable one (i.e. non-irritable, non-angry) then it really doesn't matter what our beliefs are, what our mood is, what triggered things off, how angry we got, how good we are at implementing inhibitions, and so on. In theory at any rate, you can have everything piling up against you and still make an acceptable response. And in fact it's not just theory, it can really happen in practice too.

So, if you are looking for a short cut, this is it. Personally, I wouldn't use it as a short cut, because if you *do* use it like that it is a route strewn with difficulties. If I were you I'd regard it as the final piece of the jigsaw; that way you have everything pulling on your side.

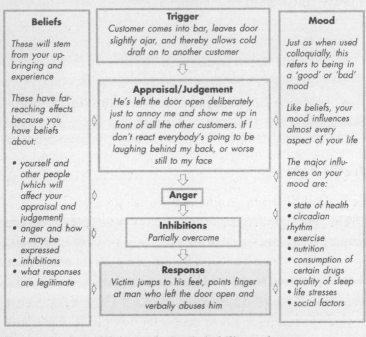

Figure 14.1 A model for analyzing irritability and anger

Either way, as far as anybody else is concerned all they can see is your response. It doesn't matter to them what's been going on inside your head; if you respond irritably and angrily then, as far as they're concerned, you are an irritable and angry person. Equally, if you respond in a non-irritable way and a non-angry way, then that is how they see you.

So, given that most of us would prefer *not* to be seen as irritable and angry, what do we do? The good news here is that we have covered most of what we need to cover already. The three key concepts are:

- the traffic lights analogy;
- modelling yourself on a good example;
- reviewing successful (and unsuccessful) incidents.

Traffic lights

Let's go through the traffic lights analogy first.

The 'red light' comes on when you can see that you are about to make an irritable and angry response – or at least, a response that will be seen by other people as irritable or angry. You treat this impulse as a red light: in other words, you literally stop. All you do is *not* say or do whatever it is you were going to say or do. If other, similar, things come into your mind, then you stay at the stop light. You get ready to move off *only* when you start thinking of alternative, non-irritable, non-angry responses.

Sometimes you can only think of one 'reasonable' response. Sometimes it takes a long time for such a response to occur to you. In that case, it simply means you are stuck on red for a long time. This is, of course, entirely true to life; just occasionally you come across lights which seem to be stuck on red for ever. But eventually, sometimes after half a second, sometimes after half a week, you think of a reasonable response. That is your cue to move on to green.

The 'green light' is simply doing whatever the reasonable response is. But remember, 'reasonable' is in *your* judgement, not the judgement of your anger. You know full well that your anger tells you to do things that the genuine *you* would disagree with. So, don't let your anger have the last word; insist that *you* do.

One of the examples we used earlier was Sue coping with her careless son Ian, who's prone to drop things and break them – mugs, for example. She describes one instance where, as soon as the mug smashed on the floor, she felt an overwhelming surge of anger; she just wanted to shout anything at him. She also describes recognizing that as a red light, and simply keeping her mouth shut for a moment. This was, more or less, a 'half-second' red light. No sooner had she come screeching to a halt on red than she quickly saw that all she needed to do was to get him to sweep it up. In other words, she moved straight on to amber, where a reasonable response occurred to her; and then on to green: 'Just sweep it up, there's a good boy,' said with the merest hint of annoyance.

The same with Chris, the character who was prone to road rage. He trained himself to recognize the red light too. He described an instance where somebody pulled in front of him rather more sharply than he felt they should have done; having braked, he literally felt his foot having a will of its own, wanting to get on to the accelerator to 'tailgate' the offender. He had by this stage of training learnt to recognize this impulse and he simply refrained from giving in to it. The 'right response' for Chris was telling himself to 'drive by his own standards'. The green light was simply doing that: taking his instruction literally, driving well and responsibly.

Following a good example

The second concept is that of modelling yourself on a good example. I have to tell you that this also is one of my very favourites. The great thing about having an example to model yourself on is that you can clearly envisage what responses you can make. All you have to do is to ask yourself: 'What would he or she do in this situation?' and you have a ready-made template for your own behavior. Then it's just a case of mimicking it.

So, by spending a couple of minutes now, you can save yourself endless hours of difficulty later on. All you need to do in that brief time is to think of somebody who would make a really good example for you. Here are a few tips to help you choose:

- You are looking for somebody, preferably the same gender as you but not necessarily, who typically makes non-irritable and non-angry responses. Someone who is difficult to get angry. Do *not* model yourself on somebody who easily becomes irritable and angry!

- It should be a person who you like, even admire; someone you would be pleased to be thought similar to.

- The individual you're modelling yourself on does not have to be 'perfect'. They may have elements to them that you would not want to copy. Even so, by and large, you like or admire them and, certainly, they are non-irritable and non-angry.
- The person you bring to mind may be someone you know from real life, or someone you know only in a public role, perhaps from television or radio. It is important, however, that you have a very vivid idea of what they say and do, so that you can copy it easily.

You might find more than one person to model yourself on. This is not necessarily a good thing, because in the heat of the moment you need to have one clear image to copy. So you're probably best off, certainly in the initial stages, having just one person to bring instantly to mind, so that you can quickly ask yourself what he or she would do in this situation.

Hence Graham (the one whose wife, Fiona, irritated him by flirting with other men) used Ian as a model. (Ian's wife, Hannah, was also something of a flirt, but only in the same harmless way as Fiona.) This was a highly appropriate model for Graham because he knew both Ian and Hannah well, recognized that Hannah had many similarities to Fiona, and could see that if only he brought himself to behave just like Ian did, then all would be well. In fact this worked out especially well because it meant that the four of them got on better than before, with each of the quartet involved effectively in 'mirroring' one another.

Paul, the father of the twelve-year-old boy who hadn't done his homework, used the character of a middle-aged teacher from a television soap opera as his model. This was an interesting one; I wasn't convinced this was a very good role-model to choose, first because this character was rather older than Paul and second because he was in fact a teacher and was therefore in a position to help youngsters with homework quite readily. Paul wasn't particularly good at his son's homework himself, so wasn't that good at helping. The third thing that slightly worried me was that this character was a bit 'too good to be true', so I was worried that Paul might be setting himself an impossible target. Happily I was proved wrong, and Paul found his role model a very good one. Even when he couldn't help his son, John, it still seemed to carry him through. Such is the power of 'modelling'.

Reviewing

You will recognize that this idea comes up time and again. Quite rightly too; it is very important indeed. This is how we really consolidate things: by reviewing both good and bad events, and taking our lessons from them.

So, if you do let yourself down at all (i.e. get too irritable and too angry) then, as soon as you have got back to your normal self, do a thorough review. What would you have preferred to do in that situation? (In other words, what response would you have preferred to make?) Would it have been best to use the traffic lights technique, the modelling technique, or to combine the two? When you combine the two you simply stop at the red light of irritability and anger, think of your role-model to help you come up with a suitable response (the amber light), and then move off to mimic that response (the green light).

So you literally relive the situation, but give it a better ending. This, technically, is known as 'cognitive rehearsal'. It is very effective because, as mentioned before, the brain can't really tell whether you're doing things in reality or in imagination. So you are treading the path through the jungle, preparing a path so that the next time a similar situation arises you're more likely to respond in the way you want to rather than in the way your habit or your anger tells you.

A NOTE OF CAUTION

There is one trap in reviewing and that is that you simply relive whatever it is that made you angry. Be careful to walk around this trap. The whole point of reviewing is to relive *a better response*. Certainly people do and say things which we would prefer they didn't do and say, but that does not mean we have to respond badly. So, we relive and practise (mentally) *the response we'd prefer to make*.

Just as important, possibly even more so, is to relive our successes. When we see something happen that would formerly have produced a really bad response from us, and yet, this time, we handle it well, then we must take time to indulge in self-congratulation. As soon as possible after the event, do a review in just the same way as if you had *not* responded as you would have wished. Again, take care to walk round the trap of simply reviewing what might have made you angry. Rather, review how you managed to respond so well as you did. You can even take it a step further and imagine various other triggers and how you would respond to them in a non-irritable, non-angry way.

SUMMARY

- In this chapter we have seen that we could, if we wished, cut through everything else to the 'bottom line': how we respond. No matter what triggers are put in our way, we are responsible for our own responses.

- There are three good ways for you to get yourself to produce the kind of responses you want to, and those three ways mesh with each other.

- First is the traffic lights technique. When you feel a surge of irritability and anger you simply stop. And you stay on 'red' until you can think of a reasonable response (from *you* rather than your anger); this is 'amber'. Once you've got that response clearly in mind you can move on to 'green' and implement it.

- Second is the technique of modelling yourself on a good example. You think of a particular person who always (so far as you know) responds well in adversity, in other words in a non-irritable, non-angry way. You hold this person in mind constantly and, when you are confronted with potential irritability- and anger-producing situations, you respond as s/he would do. Eventually this becomes part of you: you will have grafted these better responses on to the good elements of your own personality.

- Third is the technique of reviewing: instances where you responded badly and – especially – those where you responded well. In both cases you rehearse future responses where you literally envisage the potentially anger-producing stimulus (but avoid the trap of getting involved in reliving it) and rehearse the response you would prefer to make.

PROJECT

The best project from this chapter is to implement all three of the methods we have been talking about.

- Start with the traffic lights technique. Become razor-sharp at recognizing impending irritability and anger, and put yourself on red straight away. Think of the person you have set as an example to model yourself on, and what s/he would do in this situation. This puts you on to amber, because you now have a picture of a really good (non-irritable, non-angry) response. Then move on to green, in other words implement that response convincingly and with enthusiasm.
- That meshes the first two techniques. All you then need to do is to review the times you successfully implement them – and, indeed, review the times when you fail to implement them and how it should have gone. Both of these are good things to do.

This is a very solid project which will be of tremendous benefit to you if you put your heart into it.

15

'But I'm not always irritable, just sometimes': Mood

Do you ever have that experience where you just *feel* irritable? No one has even done anything yet, but you know that if they did then it would really irritate you. Or you are with other people and absolutely everything anybody says or does, and the way they do it, irritates you.

Perhaps other people don't realize you're feeling that way, perhaps you're able to keep it to yourself – possibly as a result of reading the previous chapter on 'responses'. But inside you're just feeling tremendously 'prickly'.

Colloquially, this is referred to as 'being in a bad mood', and this about sums it up. Technically, too, that feeling comes under the heading of 'mood'. Back in Part One (Chapter 7) we looked at the kind of things that influence mood, namely: routine, exercise, nutrition, drugs, sleep, illness, stress and social factors. If we can get these factors right, then we are much less likely to find ourselves in 'a bad mood' (see Figure 15.1).

Interestingly, many people have got so many of these factors awry that they spend a good deal of their lives in a bad mood, and indeed feel that this is 'part of life'. The good news is that this is not so; it's perfectly possible – and reasonably easy – to sort out these factors so that recurrent 'bad moods' become past history.

So, let's take them in turn.

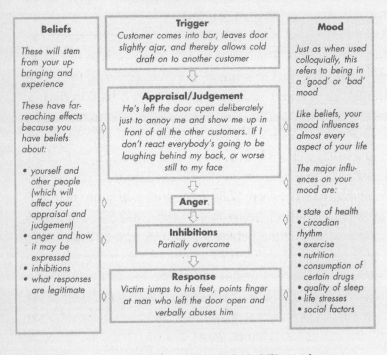

Figure 15.1   **A model for analyzing irritability and anger**

Routine

The body loves routine, doing the same things at the same time most days. Don't be tricked by the idea that 'routine' need be boring. On the contrary, you can if you wish lead the most exciting life of anybody in the world; just make sure you do it every day!

The two *main* things that the body wants to do at regular times are eating and sleeping. Of the two, sleeping is probably the more important.

So what you need to do is to go to bed and get up at roughly the same time most days.

Likewise, you need to try to eat at roughly the same times most days. The best way of doing this is to set yourself times for breakfast, lunch, tea and supper (if those are the meals you eat), and then give yourself half an hour's leeway either way. So, you might say that you eat breakfast at 8 a.m., lunch at 1 p.m., tea or snack at 5 p.m. and supper at 8 p.m., which would in fact mean that you had breakfast some time between 7.30 a.m. and 8.30 a.m., lunch at some time between 12.30 p.m. and 1.30 p.m., tea or a snack at some time between 4.30 p.m. and 5.30 p.m., and supper at some time between 7.30 p.m. and 8.30 p.m.

I labour the point because I have seen some people who become over-meticulous about eating at *exactly* the same time every day, and that can be constricting and difficult to maintain. All I am suggesting is that you eat and sleep at *roughly* the same times, most days.

And what happens if you don't? If you know what jet-lag is like, then that's what your life becomes, except that you are permanently in a state akin to jet-lag. There is nothing mystical about how jet-lag occurs: it has nothing to do with jet engines or aeroplanes in themselves, it is simply that one moves from one time zone to another, and this upsets the 'body clock', one's physical rhythm or routine.

Technically, this is known as the 'circadian rhythm' – the rhythm of regularity around a 24-hour cycle that the body likes to maintain.

And when you're in a state of jet-lag – which is often characterized as 'tired and irritable' – you are, sure enough, irritable. So, just by ensuring that you maintain a regular routine you may well massively reduce your irritability.

CIRCADIAN RHYTHM PROJECT

This all leads to a very clear and powerful project.

Step 1: List all of the following:
- Get-up time:
- First meal time:
- Second meal time:
- Third meal time:
- Fourth meal time (if any):
- Bedtime:

Step 2: Stick to the times you have written, within 30 minutes either way.

Step 3: You can make a diary of this if you want; in other words, simply record the actual times you eat and sleep. You might be surprised how difficult it is to keep them regular, especially if you're not in the habit of doing so. However, persist; this is one of the linchpins in producing a stable mood for yourself.

Taking exercise

Yes, I know you've heard it before, that exercise is very good for you. Well, I'm afraid it's entirely true: human beings are indeed designed to take exercise. It lifts the mood, strengthens up all manner of physical factors, and is generally absolute magic.

The only good news (if you are anything like me) is that exercise does not have to be strenuous. You do not necessarily have to go to a gym and 'work out'. Walking is just as effective.

Conventional wisdom says that aerobic exercise is best, but more recent research seems to suggest that any exercise is good exercise. So, walk whenever you can, run upstairs – generally just get as much exercise as you possibly can fit in. If you want to go swimming as well, or join a gym, then of course this is excellent too. But don't do any strenuous exercise without checking things out with your doctor.

A COUPLE OF TIPS

Three factors that have cropped up fairly regularly with people I have seen are as follows:

- People (especially, but not only, women) say that they would walk but they are inhibited from doing so by the wrong shoes. We are not talking about 'serious' walking; just walking to and from the bus stop, or even upstairs sometimes. Clearly there is a question of how much priority is being given to exercising here; give it a bit more priority and make sure you have shoes that are comfortable enough to walk in and, if you like, even look good as well.

- Some people, whose natural opportunities for exercise are virtually nil, say that when they get home they are too tired to exercise. The first point to make here is that if they could make themselves exercise, then the exercise itself would make them feel more energetic. The second way of looking at it (because it is in fact very difficult to 'make' yourself exercise) is again that they should give the exercise more priority: in other words, exercise earlier in the morning, at midday, or at some other time, if they know that they are going to be too tired in the evening. (And, in turn, this would make them feel less tired in the evening too.)

- Some people are tempted to mix exercise with anxiety. For example, I had one chap who deliberately set off slightly late to catch the bus every morning. This meant that he would have to walk fairly briskly down the road to the bus stop. This is a pity; exercise is meant to be an entirely natural and anxiety-free activity!

EXERCISE PROJECT

This too is a key area with massive potential benefits for you.

- The best project is simply to keep a diary of how much exercise you get. This can be 'endemic' exercise, where exercises are simply 'built into your routine' by way of walking from one place to another and so forth. In fact, to make it part and parcel of your routine is probably a very good idea; this means it won't slip once your enthusiasm wanes! Or it can be 'scheduled' exercise: deliberately going for a walk, or for a swim, or for a session in the gym.

- Either way, it is a very good idea to record how much exercise you're getting. Take it from me, it can be very salutary indeed to see just how little one sometimes gets!
- The final question is: just how much exercise *should* you get? The answer is: pretty well as much as you like. For those of us in a 'normal' routine it is very difficult to get too much exercise. Just make sure you get plenty of non-strenuous activity. To be breathing faster than normal and possibly even sweating is a good thing; to be noticeably breathless and in discomfort is not.

Nutrition

In most of the western world people certainly consume plenty of calories. But whether you get a diet that is good for you is perhaps another matter.

There often seems to be a lot of conflicting information around about what constitutes a good diet, and that sometimes means that people feel like giving up and eating whatever they feel like eating. That is a pity, because it is simple enough to get a reasonably balanced diet.

Current conventional wisdom is best summarized by saying there are four main types of foods –

1 fruit and vegetables;
2 foods such as bread, rice, potatoes;
3 high-protein foods such as meat, fish;
4 high-fat foods such as biscuits, chocolates, etc.

– and that we should eat them in that order of quantity. There is nothing 'wrong' with any of the four categories;

it's simply a matter of proportion. We should eat most of the fruit and vegetable category, least of the high-fat foods, with the others in between.

Incidentally, it is probably a mistake to actively avoid particular types of food unless you have a clearly diagnosed allergy to them – as in the case, for some people, of nuts. For instance, it can be unwise to actively avoid cholesterol, because excessively low levels of cholesterol have been shown to be associated with low mood. (But, equally, taking a moderate amount of cholesterol does *not* necessarily mean eating a lot of biscuits and chocolates; some of the best forms of cholesterol occur in oily fish such as mackerel, herring, etc.)

The next thing is: how good are you at digesting your food? No doubt you were told it as a youngster that you need to chew your food properly before swallowing – and it's still true! The reason for this is not only that digestive juices are secreted in the mouth, but that chewing also stimulates the production of other juices in the digestive tract, so that, when the food arrives there, it is 'expected'.

Similarly, it is best if you can 'put your mind to' eating, rather than eating while you are on the move, talking in too involved a way with other people, and so forth.

And finally, it is still true that most people don't drink nearly enough water. And it *is* probably best to say 'water' rather than 'fluids', even though the latter sounds so much more technical! The trouble is that if you think in terms of 'fluids' it opens the door to too much coffee, tea, etc. Best to think in terms of water. You don't have to drink any more than you want, but do drink plenty.

There's no need to go overboard on this one. Just ensure the following:

- Eat an approximately balanced diet, as described above.
- Give your body a good chance at properly digesting the food you eat by having some respect for mealtimes, food and your digestive tract! Remember, it is not so much the case that 'we are what we eat' as 'we are what we properly digest.'
- Drink plenty of water.

I say 'there's no need to go overboard' simply because I wouldn't want you to get obsessed with what you eat, how you eat it and what you drink with it. Nevertheless, nutrition is important; so, if it's especially relevant to you, make sure you sort it out.

Drugs

In this section I just want to talk about the so-called 'endemic' drugs: caffeine and alcohol. They are termed 'endemic' because they are part and parcel of everyday life as far as many people are concerned.

Caffeine is probably the bigger offender as far as disrupting mood is concerned – and a worse offender than most people think.

First of all, let's have a look where it comes from. Table 15.1 below shows us that the major sources of caffeine are coffee (including instant), tea (more or less on a par with instant coffee, which surprises many people), and cola drinks. There is also a fair amount in dark chocolate, especially if you eat lots of it!

TABLE 15.1: THE CAFFEINE CONTENT OF SOME DRINKS AND FOODS:

Item	Average caffeine content (mg)
Coffee (5 oz cup)	
brewed drip method	115
brewed percolator	80
instant	65
decaffeinated, brewed	3
decaffeinated, instant	2
Tea	
brewed (5 oz cup)	50
instant (5 oz cup)	30
iced (12 oz glass)	70
Cocoa beverage (5 oz cup)	4
Chocolate milk beverage (8 oz)	5
Milk chocolate (1 oz)	6
Dark chocolate, semi-sweet (1 oz)	20
Coca-Cola (12 oz)	45.6
Diet Coke	45.6
Pepsi Cola	38.4
Diet Pepsi	36
Pepsi Light	36

Some weight-control aids, alertness tablets and diuretics also contain significant amounts of caffeine.

Source: US Food and Drugs Administration.

Both caffeine and alcohol are listed as substances which produce substance-related mood disorders in the American Psychiatric Association's *Diagnostic and Statistical Manual* (4th edition, 1994). It comes as a surprise to many people that caffeine can have the far-reaching effects it does. It has been shown to be associated with low birthweight for babies from high caffeine-consuming mothers and an increased risk of cardiac problems in high caffeine-consuming people; and of course it is known for its sleep-disturbance properties and the 'jittery' effect that many people have when they drink too much.

In summary, caffeine is one of those substances that is best taken strictly in moderation. There is some evidence that at such a level (around three cups of instant coffee per day) it has quite a good anti-depressant effect; much more and you really need to be cutting down, back to around that daily level of three cups.

If you are drinking an excessive amount of coffee (and I've come across people who drink thirty cups a day), the best way of cutting down is first of all to halve your current consumption. Then hold that level steady for a week or two. Then halve it again. Then hold that level for a week or two, and halve it again if necessary – keeping going until you get to around three cups a day.

You may well find it surprisingly difficult to cut back because, although most people don't think they are addicted to the amount of caffeine they consume, you probably are. Common withdrawal symptoms include painful headaches and tiredness, although in total it appears that caffeine depletes your energy levels rather than boosts them. Some people who have headaches first thing in the morning or at weekends find that they are associated with caffeine withdrawal because, naturally enough, one doesn't normally consume caffeine through the night and many people drink a lot more caffeine during the working week than at weekends.

In summary, then, limit yourself to around three cups of instant coffee or its equivalent each day. And even then, don't have one of those in the evening time or it will probably interfere with your sleep.

Pretty much the same applies to alcohol. In moderation it's fine, but in excess it really is troublesome.

Recommended weekly maxima in the UK are currently 21 units for men and 14 units for women, where a unit is roughly equivalent to a glass of wine, half a pint of beer or a measure of spirits. Current US recommendations are for a slightly lower intake; the Connecticut Clearinghouse ('a program of Wheeler Clinic Inc., funded by the Department of Mental Health and Addictions Service') says that 'moderate drinking' should not be exceeded, and defines 'moderate' intake as one drink a day for females and two drinks a day for males, where one drink is equivalent to 1.5 ounces of distilled spirit (80% proof), 5 ounces of wine or 12 ounces of regular beer.

Personally, although I confess to being rather fond of drinking, I expect that the UK maxima will be lowered in due course. Anyway, if you drink much more than this and also find yourself troubled by irritability, then you really need to work hard at getting down to these limits as a maximum.

The real problem with alcohol is that it interferes with your sleep. Contrary to popular belief, the chances are that your quality of sleep is actually impaired rather than improved by consuming alcohol. Obviously, taken in large amounts it leaves you hung over, and taken even in not very great amounts it still leaves you under par the next day, partly because it attacks your supply of B vitamins.

It's no real answer, but if you are drinking too much alcohol and find it very difficult to cut it down to reasonable levels, then at least make sure that you take regular multivitamin supplements. Clearly this is not half as good as not damaging yourself in the first place, but it does go some way to undoing part of the damage.

ALCOHOL PROJECT

- This one is clear and simple: get down to the recommended maxima of alcohol per week.
- Obviously this is a very important one, not only because of the implications for your irritability, but also in terms of minimizing the damage alcohol does to your liver and brain especially.
- If you can manage this by yourself, simply by starting up a new habit of drinking a lot less, then so much to the good. If you need some outside help, it's worth getting it. Your family doctor might be able to recommend somebody, or you can get in touch with Alcoholics Anonymous (local contact numbers are in the phone book); you don't have to be drinking as much as you think in order to get help from them.

Recreational ('street') drugs

This category covers a great many drugs, and I am not expert on any of them, so I don't propose to say too much here. I would rather leave it to your own judgement. Given what we have said above about the 'routine' drugs of caffeine and alcohol and the damaging effects that they have been proved to inflict upon us, you can probably judge for yourself what effect other drugs might be having on you, if you are taking any, and what you had best do about it!

Sleep

The importance of sleep is very difficult to overstate. If you can get into the routine of having a good night's sleep, then this will have a major impact on the quality of your mood. There are a number of rules, many of which have been mentioned already:

- Get up at a regular time; the body likes routine.
- Eat at regular times; again, the body likes routine.
- Avoid too much caffeine (not more than around three cups of instant coffee per day) and too much alcohol (not more than three units per day if you are a man, two if you're a woman).
- Get a reasonable amount of physical and mental activity into your day; try to break the vicious circle of feeling tired, therefore not doing much, therefore not sleeping very well and therefore feeling tired . . .

- Have a wind-down period before you go to bed; a low-activity routine so that you go to bed relaxed.
- Make sure you're neither too hungry nor too full when you go to bed.
- Ensure that you have a regular bedtime; again, the body likes routine.
- Some people find they are able to induce a state of happiness as they lie in bed; if you can do this it's a good idea – happy people sleep better than unhappy ones!
- Make sure you've got rid of any extraneous sudden noises from central heating or anything else, and that you are warm enough but not too hot.

Well, that isn't exactly a fully comprehensive account of how to reform your sleeping habits, but it's a fair start. If you really make sure that you are doing all of those, all at once, then you shouldn't be sleeping too badly at all. Only one other thing; don't *try* to sleep – even if you just lie there awake but relaxed all night your brain will go into a different mode and you'll have a reasonable amount of rest, so long as you don't actually harass yourself with trying to sleep.

SLEEP PROJECT

- Regardless of whether you think of yourself as having sleep problems it is still an excellent idea to get as good a night's sleep as possible. The importance of a good night's sleep is very difficult to overestimate.

- Therefore apply your mind to implementing as many of the above points as you can, including setting realistic times for bedtime and getting-up time in order to ensure that you have enough time in bed but not too much.

- Of course, if you work shifts, this can be a tremendous problem. Some people seem to be able to manage shift work quite easily, others not. In either case do make sure that you get straight into the new routine as soon as your shift changes; the body isn't normally too upset about occasional changes in the routine so long as you then stick to it for a substantial period of time. Other people simply cannot tolerate, for example, night-shift work. If you are one of those then you might have to take more radical measures like moving on to a job that doesn't entail night-working.

- Come what may, make sure you do everything in your power to get a good night's sleep.

Illness

If you are going through a period of illness, then the chances are that this will affect your mood.

There may not, of course, be a lot you can do about this. Let's assume, in any event, that you are doing all you can in terms of overcoming the illness, regardless of whether it's short-term or long-term, physical or mental.

What we are interested in here is your levels of, and tendency towards, irritability and anger. In that respect there is one major thing you can do: namely, when you find a person who's irritating you and you suspect it may be because of your illness, make sure you lay the blame fair and square on your *illness*, not on the *person*. If you want to swear and curse at anything, do it at the illness rather than the person. And, that being the case, make sure it's under your breath!

There is a very important general rule here: it is always good to lay the blame fair and square where it belongs rather than dumping it on some poor unfortunate who happens to be nearby!

There is just one illness I'd like us to look at more carefully, because it is so often associated with irritability and anger. And that illness is a mental one, namely depression.

Depression

My friend and colleague Paul Gilbert has written an extremely good book on *Overcoming Depression* in this series. However, just for the moment, rather than embark on reading a completely new book, allow me to give you a few tips. That is all they are; but just see if any of these fits your needs.

- Think less, do more. Thinking is one of the great traps in depression. Many people, when they find themselves feeling low, indulge in two types of unhelpful thinking. First, they dwell on and brood over their problems; and second, they 'introspect' – in other words, they think too much about where they might be going wrong. As a general rule, too much thinking doesn't do us any good. Effectively, it digs us deeper into the swamp we are trying to climb out of. Action, on the other hand, is usually helpful. It doesn't particularly matter what the action is. Doing things of any sort seems to be a good idea.

- Envisage a future you want. Regardless of whether you are thinking short-term or long-term, next weekend or ten years hence, looking forward to a good future is a powerful antidepressant. Have a clear picture of what it is you want; write it down or draw pictures of what you're after. But whatever you do, make sure that you have really clear images of the future that you want and how you might obtain it. And do it regularly; it's not a 'once and for all' activity.

- When you do think, be careful what you think *about*. Sometimes people spend time thinking about things that make them unhappy. Sometimes the connection is obvious – thinking about sad things makes most people unhappy. Sometimes it is less obvious; you might, for example, spend time thinking about a good relationship you used to have, but when you stop thinking about it find that you have become unhappy. Try to be aware of what effect your thoughts have on you, and spend less time thinking about things that make you unhappy and more time thinking about things that make you happy.

- Get yourself a good routine with plenty of exercise and sleep, good nutrition, and limited unhelpful drugs. We have probably said enough about this one, but if you get all those things right you're off to a terrific start.

- Act as if you are happy and relaxed. The way we walk, sit, stand and talk gives signals to the brain about how we are. So, it's a good idea to send 'non-depressed' signals to the brain. Try an experiment if you want. Normally, if you're feeling down, you'll be sitting in a depressed kind of way. If somebody came in and saw you, they'd say you *looked* depressed. So, right now, sit in a non-depressed way. Very quickly, almost immediately, you'll feel the difference. It is very difficult to sit non-depressed and yet *feel* depressed. If you act *as if* you're perfectly happy and relaxed, your brain will, to a degree, follow your lead.

- Have a *good day*. Life consists of a series of days; if you can make each one reasonably good, then you will have a rewarding life. Of course, most days involve some things we don't really want to do and other things we do want to do. The best slogan here is: 'Do the worst first.' That way you're always on the 'downhill run', each thing leading on to something better. If you do it the other way round, you are constantly being 'punished' for everything you do. Also, beware of trying to plan things that will make you happy: you are probably on to a loser here. Happiness is an elusive quality: the more you chase it, the more it runs away from you. It's maybe better to plan things that you think are 'right' or possibly even things that will 'make you feel good about yourself'.

- Sort out your environment. Sometimes when I call on people who have been depressed for a while, I look at where they live and think it's no wonder they're depressed. Any reasonable person, living there, would be depressed. And it's not usually anything to do with money; it's just a badly organized environment. There are three key principles: (1) have things so you feel safe (you're not going to trip up, electrocute yourself, bump into sharp corners, etc.); (2) have things so you are comfortable (chairs, bed, table, work surfaces); (3) have things around you that you like and that make you feel good (specific furniture, pictures, colours, etc.). Take this further if you want. Watch and listen to television and radio programmes that make you feel good rather than bad. Listen to music that makes you feel upbeat rather than down, and so on.

- Sort out your social life. Most people are social beings, so it's important to have this area reasonably well sorted. In the first place, intimate relationships are very important to us, so if you have one it's important to do your level best to make it as good as it can be. Work at developing a good relationship with your partner. For some people this isn't very good, but just get it to its maximum! One word of warning: if you are depressed, you tend to be depressed with your partner (in just the same way as you're probably also depressed with your house, job, car, etc.). This does not mean that your partner is necessarily *causing* your depression. Of course, s/he may be; but be cautious, think carefully before you do or say anything too precipitate.

- Non-intimate relationships are important too. Make them as good as you can. But make them 'real' relationships. In other words, to paraphrase President Kennedy, 'Ask not what your friends can do for you, but what you can do for your friends.' Humans have a rather good design feature whereby if you follow that maxim, your friends benefit a lot *and so do you*. It's a question of cultivating a real interest in your friends rather than 'using them' to provide yourself with a social life.

- 'Gentle up' on yourself. Sometimes people can be really hard on themselves when they are depressed. In fact, sometimes it is the act of being so hard on themselves that causes the depression. They make rules for themselves that are rigid, extreme and over-generalized, rules like: 'I've got to be loved by everybody,' and 'I've got to be 100 per cent perfect in everything I do,' and 'It's terrible if things aren't just the way I want them to be.' To lighten up on yourself, soften these rules to: 'It is nice to have some people who like me (but I can't be liked by everybody,' 'It is nice to do things right (but sometimes things are less than perfect),' 'I'd sooner have things go the way I want them (but then again, that's not always the way life is).' The rules we make for ourselves are often almost unconscious, so sometimes we really have to work hard on softening them up.

DEPRESSION PROJECT

- If you feel you are depressed and your irritability is caused by your depression, then clearly what you need to do is to sort your depression out.
- The points listed above are probably highly relevant for you. You need to go about tackling them methodically. In other words, choose just one of the factors above and really go to town on that one for the next week or two. And then choose another, and then another, until you've covered all the ones that you feel are relevant to you. This is a good major project because clearly it will make you happier and less irritable. Indeed, it can be little short of life-transforming.
- If you want to do a more comprehensive job on your depression, then embark on Paul Gilbert's *Overcoming Depression* (Robinson Publishing, revised edition, 2000) or David D. Burns's *The Feeling Good Handbook* (Plume Publishing, 1990), both of which are excellent guides to escaping from depression.
- Alternatively (or in addition), you can also go along to your doctor and get antidepressants, if you haven't already got them. Modern-day antidepressants are absolutely excellent, and very often you can get the best effect by combining antidepressants with a psychological intervention like that described above or those outlined in the books I've recommended.
- In any case, it's an absolute shame for you to go through life depressed, so set yourself a real project to resolve it. It can be done, even if you've been depressed for ages.

A TIP

Remember, whether your illness is depression or some other afflic-
tion, maybe a physical condition, develop the habit whenever
you feel irritable of *blaming the illness*, not the person who seems
to be causing the irritation.

Life stresses

Stressful life events come in at least two sorts: repetitive
stresses such as overwork; and 'once off' events such as
bereavement and divorce. Both can affect our mood substan-
tially.

Let's take the repetitive stresses first of all. We are talking
here about things such as overwork, demanding family
members (such as difficult children, or having to look after
an ageing parent), or demanding friends who need your
attention. Any one of these can become overwhelming; or
pressure from two or more together can add up to the point
where it has a serious effect on your mood.

There are three things you can do:

- reduce the stresses;
- learn to cope with the stresses better;
- view the stresses in a different light.

We'll look at these briefly in turn in a moment, but before
we do there is one other important point to be made. Again,

as with illness, if you are feeling irritable because you are 'stressed out', make sure you put the blame fairly and squarely where it belongs, in other words, on the stresser: overwork, or whatever it happens to be. Don't displace it on to whoever happens to be closest to hand.

Take Ken, for example, our stressed-out executive. Ken is under stress because of his work, not his home life. Even so, because he's stressed, when he goes home to his wife Trish, he is irritable. This means that almost anything that Trish does irritates Ken, not because *she is irritating* but because *he is irritable*. So Ken had to learn to snap *not* at Trish but at his workload. He did this rather clumsily at first. Trish would say something like: 'What should we do for dinner tonight?' and Ken, rather than replying 'I don't care,' in an irritable way, had to teach himself to say: 'All the stuff going on at work is getting me down.' This was pretty strange to Trish at first, because it is a rather odd reply to 'What should we do for dinner tonight?' Nevertheless, Ken got better at it, and eventually was able to say it quietly to himself – making the point that he was stressed out not by Trish but by his work. Further down the line he reduced his work pressures, which was of course the long-term solution.

What I'm trying to say is: blame what deserves to be blamed, rather than the person in front of you. Then, better still, sort out the underlying problem.

So, here goes. The first course of action was to *reduce the stresses*. Most people's first response to this is 'easier said than done', and there is some truth in that. For example, one woman I saw, Alison, had her mother living a few doors down from her, and the mother for very good reasons needed frequent attention. Alison said there was no way that she could give her mother any less attention than she did, so how could she possibly reduce the pressures on her? And she seemed to be correct; her mother really did seem to need the attention described. However, as we talked I learnt that Alison was (a) holding down a fairly demanding job, (b) coming home to a husband and two children and setting about making a traditional evening meal from scratch, and (c) then going off to give her mother the attention she needed. In fact, she also managed to fit in a brief visit to her mother between coming home and setting about making the meal.

So, although she had to continue to give her mother the same amount of attention, Alison could reduce the pressures on herself in other areas. She chose to cut down on the sheer amount of work involved in making the meal. She couldn't quite bring herself to delegate it to her husband, but she did go for convenience food and that brought her total workload down to a manageable level.

STRESS PROJECT (1)

- If you know you're being 'stressed out' by too many pressures, examine the total pressures you are under and do anything you can to reduce that total. The principal pressure may be unalterable, or alterable only to a small degree. Don't be put off by that, work on some of the other pressures you are under.

- Also, beware of blocking yourself by *assuming* that the major pressure is unalterable. Frequently, it isn't, even when it seems to be. Do some careful analysis and see where you can de-stress yourself.

The second course of action we looked at was *learning to cope with stresses better*. By this I mean you don't change the number or quantity of stresses affecting you; you simply act differently.

I feel that here I should start telling you about time management, self-instructional training and so forth. On the other hand, I don't know enough about what particular stresses *you* are under to make such a discussion directly relevant to you. So I will just suggest this:

- try to clarify in your mind exactly what the stresses are (which can be more difficult than at first sight seems);
- then ask several people you know how they cope with those stresses.

For example:

- If you get stressed out by putting two youngsters to bed, neither of whom wants to go and both of whom are liable to be naughty in a hundred and one different ways, ask someone else you know how they cope with it. It doesn't have to be a contemporary of yours, though it can be if you prefer; it might be someone rather older who knows what they would do 'if they had their time again'.
- If you are stressed out by having three deadlines to meet and being aware that it is impossible to meet

all three, ask somebody else who finds themselves in a similar situation what they do.

- If you are stressed out by having an overenergetic friend who always wants to drag you off to the latest new and exciting place, ask somebody else in a similar situation how they cope with that. Again, it does not have to be an exact parallel. The person you ask might have a friend who is always burdening them with their problems, but has found a method for coping with that. Maybe you could still tailor their solution to your own situation.

- If you are stressed out by being jobless, wanting a job and having too much time on your hands, again ask other people in the same situation how they cope. Possibly, just possibly, you might be able to put together a solution from the various answers you receive.

STRESS PROJECT (2)

If you feel this is a relevant area for you, do your own 'research project' on how you might cope better with the stresses affecting you. This method hinges on:

- being able to identify very clearly what it is that is stressing you;
- being able to conduct a 'survey' of one or more people who might be able to offer you a solution or a partial solution;
- putting together a personal plan that suits your own situation;
- having the determination to implement that personal plan.

The third solution we had to life's stresses was to *view them in a different way.*

Perhaps you'll excuse a personal example. Just now, even as I write this, I know that I am past the deadline for submitting this book. In fact, I am passed the third deadline set by the publisher, and I think her patience is wearing thin. But then, I can't worry too much about that because I have a whole string of people who would like me to run training courses for their organizations, and I know I am going to disappoint some of them. And then, having faced the wrath of the publisher about this book, and disappointed people who want me to run training courses, I know I'm still way behind on writing up three medico-legal reports (reports where I have interviewed a patient and am submitting my professional opinion to the court).

So, if I had any sense at all I should be completely stressed out, pulled in three directions at once – quite apart from all the 'little extras', like a journalist just having phoned up wanting to know if I have any opinions as to why knitting has suddenly taken off in popularity, what is therapeutic about it and why women do it more than men . . .

And, of course, there *is* a part of me that feels stressed by all of that. But not a very big part, because most of me is thoroughly delighted that (a) a publisher will give me money just for saying I will write a book, (b) so many people are keen for me to run courses for their organizations, and (c) so many solicitors want me to give my opinion on their clients. The knitting question is quite interesting too!

As I'm sure you know, this is known as 'reframing', which simply means seeing the same situation from a different viewpoint. All the 'stresses' are still there, just as they were previously; it's just that they're not viewed as stresses any longer, they're viewed as compliments.

The hurdle you have to get over to use this strategy is that there is a little voice in the back of the head that says you shouldn't be so 'complacent' – in my case, that really I *should* be stressed out by all the things I haven't done and work my socks off until I have caught up. Well, possibly; but the argument against *that* is that such stress is actually counter-productive and means you work less well and achieve what you're trying to achieve more slowly and less successfully.

Let's have another example. I have a friend who has a soft spot for Bangladesh. He has a tremendous amount of empathy for the Bangladeshis and the sufferings they endure by way of floods, storms and winds. He is constantly devastated by the number of people who lose their lives in the country, the amount of suffering that goes on there, and he sends regular sums of money to aid programmes associated with Bangladesh.

However, he is far from solemn about this serious concern, and whenever he hits a problem, says: 'Compared with the problems they have in Bangladesh, this is no problem at all.' And, although he says it in a flippant kind of way, it clearly has a major impact on his thinking. It is his way of 'reframing' his own problems.

Obviously, this is simply a variant on the time-honoured admonition, 'There are plenty of people worse off than you.' However, it is a very good variant for my friend because it is so much more specific. My friend really does envisage in his own mind trying to explain his problem to somebody in Bangladesh, and how minor and trivial his own problem would seem to them. Very convincing reframing.

REFRAMING PROJECT

- Reframing is a very powerful tool if you can get into it. It has the power to transform a situation quickly and permanently, if you're prepared to undertake it.
- Use the examples given above to see if there's a parallel in your own situation. How could you reframe your own situation?
- Note: This is not just an intellectual exercise! Once you have worked out how it is possible to reframe your own situation you then have to go ahead and *do it*. Get yourself in the habit of seeing your situation from this new viewpoint.

Social factors

Being social animals, we humans are greatly affected in our moods by how our social lives are progressing.

There are three major areas we have to consider:

- our most intimate relationships: with our partners if we are adults, more probably with peers, parents or carers if we are children.
- social relationships at work or wherever we occupy ourselves;
- social relationships outside of intimate and work ones, namely with friends, neighbours, etc.

To maintain a good long-term mood we need to nurture each of these three areas as best we can: not just 'using' other people to provide ourselves with a social life, but taking a genuine interest in others to give ourselves a solid social foundation.

Inevitably, however, things go wrong in one area or another. For example, you might have trouble with your relationships at work – with your boss, with colleagues, with clients, or whoever. The most common mistake in this instance is to come home and be snappy with those at home. In other words, you transfer problems from one area into a second area, immediately doubling the problem.

An alternative habit is just as easy to get into. We have to take it as given that problems do sometimes arise, so that, inevitably, there will sometimes be difficulties in relationships at work, for example. It is then a question of disciplining ourselves to switch into a different 'gear' when we get home: a gear that appreciates the support of those with whom we live, or at least one that takes us into a totally different mode at home from that prevailing at work.

And the same applies the other way round: There are sometimes problems at home that don't need to be transferred to work or friendships. When one area temporarily goes down, we need to make sure we don't contaminate the other two areas.

This is exactly the trap that Georgina was walking into. She was the teenager who was depressed and irritable because she had repeated problems with her boyfriends:

so, at home, she would be snappy with her parents and her brother because of the 'boyfriend trouble'. In this way she was alienating the very people who would naturally have provided her with support.

Georgina was a particularly interesting instance to me because she grasped this concept straight away. This was very satisfying to me as a therapist, because I could see the immediate impact of her recognition. Immediately Georgina realized what she was doing, she acted upon the idea that the times when she was sad about her boyfriend situation were the very times when she should put *more* energy into her (good) domestic situation, and the good relationships she had with other friends.

SOCIAL PROJECT

The project in this area has two parts.

- First, if necessary, build your social support in the three areas of intimate relationships, work relationships (if you go to work) and relationships outside of work and intimacy, such as those with neighbours and other friends.
- Second, be constantly aware of the trap of displacing trouble from one of the three areas into another and thereby doubling or trebling your trouble. Skirt your way round this trap by acting upon the realization that when you have trouble in one of the three areas, this is the very time to lean on and nurture the other two areas.

SUMMARY

This has been a big chapter that has looked at the all-pervasive influence of our mood on irritability and anger. It is fluctuations in mood that lead to the unpleasant effect of 'just feeling irritable' with no apparent trigger. In fact, when you feel irritable, almost anything can trigger off irritation.

But mood is not random. You can work to produce a good, stable mood by achieving the following:

- Develop a good circadian rhythm or daily routine, particularly in respect of eating and sleeping at regular times.
- Take exercise – any exercise!
- Eat a balanced diet, eat it well, and drink plenty of water.
- Go easy on caffeine (around three cups of instant coffee per day), alcohol (up to 21 units per week if you're a man, 14 if you're a woman), nicotine and other 'recreational' drugs.
- Develop a pattern of sound, refreshing sleep.
- If your irritable mood is due to illness, it's a question of clearing up the illness if possible, and if not then making sure you blame your irritability on the illness rather than on the people around you.
- Reduce the stressful effect of life stresses by (a) removing one or more of the stresses – not always the most obvious one; (b) learning to cope with the stresses better, including by asking others how they cope with them; and/or (c) reframing the stresses.
- Nurture the three key areas in your social life and, when you have trouble in one of the three areas, ensure that you don't spread it to the other two.

PROJECT

- A lot of individual projects have been set out in the course of this chapter. Your task now is an enjoyable one: read through the chapter, decide which are the most relevant areas for you, and undertake the project(s) described under that area.

- Raising your mood is a terrific task to undertake and a very rewarding one indeed. Not only will it make you less irritable, it will permanently brighten up everything around you!

16

Testing your knowledge

By this stage we have covered all the theory in Part One, and all the techniques for resolving irritability and anger in Part Two. Now it's just a question of applying all this knowledge!

Perhaps you have already applied crucial elements of the programme to your own situation and made some good progress. Or maybe you are planning to set about this in a short while. Either way, it's time now to test yourself out on other people's problems and see how you get on.

To do this, constantly bear in mind the model we have developed, shown again here in Figure 16.1. Use that model to recommend to each of the following people what they should do, as described in the exercise.

Exercise

Below is a list of people, all of whom have problems with irritability and anger. Which of the options covered in Part Two of this book, and summarized here, would you recommend to each of them? You may choose to recommend more than one option for each problem.

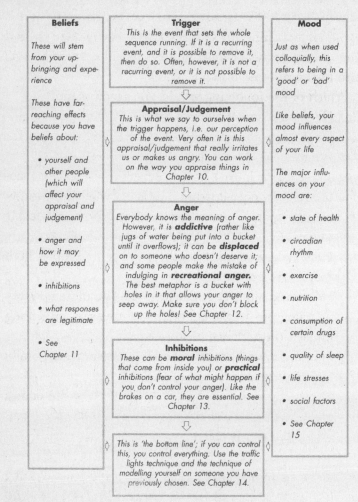

Beliefs

These will stem from your up-bringing and experience

These have far-reaching effects because you have beliefs about:

- yourself and other people (which will affect your appraisal and judgement)

- anger and how it may be expressed

- inhibitions

- what responses are legitimate

- See Chapter 11

Trigger
This is the event that sets the whole sequence running. If it is a recurring event, and it is possible to remove it, then do so. Often, however, it is not a recurring event, or it is not possible to remove it.

Appraisal/Judgement
This is what we say to ourselves when the trigger happens, i.e. our perception of the event. Very often it is this appraisal/judgement that really irritates us or makes us angry. You can work on the way you appraise things in Chapter 10.

Anger
Everybody knows the meaning of anger. However, it is **addictive** (rather like jugs of water being put into a bucket until it overflows); it can be **displaced** on to someone who doesn't deserve it; and some people make the mistake of indulging in **recreational anger.** The best metaphor is a bucket with holes in it that allows your anger to seep away. Make sure you don't block up the holes! See Chapter 12.

Inhibitions
These can be **moral** inhibitions (things that come from inside you) or **practical** inhibitions (fear of what might happen if you don't control your anger). Like the brakes on a car, they are essential. See Chapter 13.

This is 'the bottom line'; if you can control this, you control everything. Use the traffic lights technique and the technique of modelling yourself on someone you have previously chosen. See Chapter 14.

Mood

Just as when used colloquially, this refers to being in a 'good' or 'bad' mood

Like beliefs, your mood influences almost every aspect of your life

The major influences on your mood are:

- state of health

- circadian rhythm

- exercise

- nutrition

- consumption of certain drugs

- quality of sleep

- life stresses

- social factors

- See Chapter 15

Figure 16.1 A model for analyzing irritability and anger

1 Gerry has noisy next-door neighbours who repeatedly play their music too loud. Over the last three or four months this has made him angrier and angrier until he can hardly

control himself. He is now sensitized to the noise and is constantly listening for it. If he has his own stereo on and then thinks he hears loud music from next door he will turn his own stereo down to check.

Which of the following would you recommend?

(a) He should somehow remove the trigger.
(b) He should alter his appraisal and judgement of the situation so that he sees it in a different way.
(c) The trouble is that he is displacing his anger inappropriately, not allowing it to leak away fast enough, or indulging in recreational anger. He should tackle this.
(d) He should work at strengthening his inhibitions, both moral and practical.
(e) He should alter his response to the situation, possibly by using the 'traffic lights' technique or by modelling himself on someone he knows.
(f) He should work on his beliefs, it is these that are really making him angry and irritable.
(g) He should work on his mood; sometimes he is in a good mood and sometimes he is in a bad mood and this is the real problem.

2 Colin is really irritated by his neighbours' kids playing football in the street outside his house. Often the ball will go across his lawn and sometimes it even hits his windows. Just like Gerry, he has become increasingly incensed over time and is now constantly on the look-out for the football games to start. His anger is now at a high level and is almost constantly with him.

Which of the following would you recommend?

(a) He should somehow remove the trigger.

(b) He should alter his appraisal and judgement of the situation so that he sees it in a different way.

(c) He is displacing his anger inappropriately, not allowing it to leak away fast enough, or indulging in recreational anger. He should tackle this.

(d) He should work at strengthening his inhibitions, both moral and practical.

(e) He should alter his response to the situation, possibly by using the 'traffic lights' technique or by modelling himself on someone he knows.

(f) He should work on his beliefs, it is these that are really making him angry and irritable.

(g) He should work on his mood; sometimes he is in a good mood and sometimes he is in a bad mood and this is the real problem.

3 Steve 'blows his top' much more often than he should do. For an example, he tells you about the evening when he was sitting in a bar, near the door, with his friends Ben and Chris. During the course of the evening several people came into the bar and left the door ajar. As it was a cold November evening, each time this happened Steve, Ben and Chris were left in a draft. As the evening wore on, Steve got gradually more angry during the evening until, when a fifth person came in and left the door open, he jumped up and laid into him verbally. However, Steve says this is just one instance of many; he says he's always a bit prone to behave like this, but some days he is much worse than others.

Which of the following would you recommend?

(a) He should somehow remove the trigger.

(b) He should alter his appraisal and judgement of the situation so that he sees it in a different way.

(c) The trouble is that he is displacing his anger inappropriately, not allowing it to leak away fast enough, or indulging in recreational anger. He should tackle this.

(d) He should work at strengthening his inhibitions, both moral and practical.

(e) He should alter his response to the situation, possibly by using the 'traffic lights' technique or by modelling himself on someone he knows.

(f) He should work on his beliefs, it is these that are really making him angry and irritable.

(g) He should work on his mood; sometimes he is in a good mood and sometimes he is in a bad mood and this is the real problem.

4   Pam is intensely annoyed by the noise her husband makes when he eats his food. She used to tell him about it, but it seems to have made no difference and she has now given up. The trouble is that now it has come to symbolize what she sees as their incompatibility. Just like Gerry and Colin, she is now sensitized to the noise he makes and almost waits for it at each mealtime. And in truth the pair do seem to be incompatible.

Which of the following would you recommend?

(a) She should somehow remove the trigger.

(b) She should alter her appraisal and judgement of the situation so that she sees it in a different way.

(c) The trouble is that she is displacing her anger inappropriately, not allowing it to leak away fast enough, or indulging in recreational anger. She should tackle this.

(d) She should work at strengthening her inhibitions, both moral and practical.

(e) She should alter her response to the situation, possibly by using the 'traffic lights' technique or by modelling herself on someone she knows.

(f) She should work on her beliefs, it is these that are really making her angry and irritable.

(g) She should work on her mood; sometimes she is in a good mood and sometimes she is in a bad mood and this is the real problem.

5 Sue says that her son, Ian, drives her mad. She gives an example of how, recently, he dropped a mug on the kitchen floor and broke it, which caused her to completely 'lose it' with him. But she says this is just one example of thousands. She thinks he is careless, but even so she is embarrassed by her overreaction to what she knows are relatively minor events. She also says that on some days she is worse than others.

Which of the following would you recommend?

(a) She should somehow remove the trigger.

(b) She should alter her appraisal and judgement of the situation so that she sees it in a different way.

(c) The trouble is that she is displacing her anger inappropriately, not allowing it to leak away fast enough, or indulging in recreational anger. She should tackle this.

(d) She should work at strengthening her inhibitions, both moral and practical.

(e) She should alter her response to the situation, possibly by using the 'traffic lights' technique or by modelling herself on someone she knows.

(f) She should work on her beliefs, it is these that are really making her angry and irritable.

(g) She should work on her mood; sometimes she is in a good mood and sometimes she is in a bad mood and this is the real problem.

6 Nigel repeatedly gets angry with his wife, though he does not always vent that anger. The main thing that causes him to become angry is when she contradicts him in public. Frequently the level of these contradictions is very minor (for example, whether a particular event happened on a Wednesday or a Tuesday). It is the contradiction itself that really gets to him. He can see that in many ways this is a minor thing, and on the one hand feels that he is behaving rather 'childishly' to become so uptight about it. On the other hand he is worried that maybe in some ways his feelings are indicative of something 'deeper' that should be sorted out.

Which of the following would you recommend?

(a) He should somehow remove the trigger.

(b) He should alter his appraisal and judgement of the situation so that he sees it in a different way.

(c) The trouble is that he is displacing his anger inappropriately, not allowing it to leak away fast enough, or indulging in recreational anger. He should tackle this.

(d) He should work at strengthening his inhibitions, both moral and practical.

(e) He should alter his response to the situation, possibly by using the 'traffic lights' technique or by modelling himself on someone he knows.

(f) He should work on his beliefs, it is these that are really making him angry and irritable.

(g) He should work on his mood; sometimes he is in a good mood and sometimes he is in a bad mood and this is the real problem.

7 Alan, an electrician, is repeatedly incensed by his boss asking him to do 'one more job'. He feels he is being 'put-upon' and taken advantage of. He has never said anything to his boss for fear of harming his future career prospects. Also, there is a part of him that wonders if he is making too much of it; he thinks maybe most people might not be quite as angry as he is if they were in the same situation. In other words, he is concerned he is overreacting. This is slightly paradoxical inasmuch as his boss knows nothing of Alan's inner fury.

Which of the following would you recommend?

(a) He should somehow remove the trigger.

(b) He should alter his appraisal and judgement of the situation so that he sees it in a different way.

(c) The trouble is that he is displacing his anger inappropriately, not allowing it to leak away fast enough, or indulging in recreational anger. He should tackle this.

(d) He should work at strengthening his inhibitions, both moral and practical.

(e) He should alter his response to the situation, possibly by using the 'traffic lights' technique or by modelling himself on someone he knows.

(f) He should work on his beliefs, it is these that are really making him angry and irritable.

(g) He should work on his mood; sometimes he is in a good mood and sometimes he is in a bad mood and this is the real problem.

8 Georgina, who is seventeen, sometimes gets very depressed and irritable because of 'boyfriend trouble'. She would very much like to be in a stable relationship, but only has occasional boyfriends. This upsets her and she takes it out on her family and friends. They see her as 'moody' and a very irritable young lady. Gradually this has driven many of her friends away.

Which of the following would you recommend?

(a) She should somehow remove the trigger.

(b) She should alter her appraisal and judgement of the situation so that she sees it in a different way.

(c) The trouble is that she is displacing her anger inappropriately, not allowing it to leak away fast enough, or indulging in recreational anger. She should tackle this.

(d) She should work at strengthening her inhibitions, both moral and practical.

(e) She should alter her response to the situation, possibly by using the 'traffic lights' technique or by modelling herself on someone she knows.

(f) She should work on her beliefs, it is these that are really making her angry and irritable.

(g) She should work on her mood; sometimes she is in a good mood and sometimes she is in a bad mood and this is the real problem.

9 Danny and Vicky are both well-known figures in the public eye. Danny sometimes gets very angry with Vicky because she says things about their private life which he views as best left unsaid in public.
   Which of the following would you recommend?
   (a) He should somehow remove the trigger.
   (b) He should alter his appraisal and judgement of the situation so that he sees it in a different way.
   (c) The trouble is that he is displacing his anger inappropriately, not allowing it to leak away fast enough, or indulging in recreational anger. He should tackle this.
   (d) He should work at strengthening his inhibitions, both moral and practical.
   (e) He should alter his response to the situation, possibly by using the 'traffic lights' technique or by modelling himself on someone he knows.
   (f) He should work on his beliefs, it is these that are really making him angry and irritable.
   (g) He should work on his mood; sometimes he is in a good mood and sometimes he is in a bad mood and this is the real problem.

10 Graham is intensely irritated by his wife, Fiona, flirting with other men – the more so because their friend Ian doesn't seem to be bothered at all by his wife, Hannah, flirting.

Nevertheless, it really gets to Graham and he now sees this as a real problem which is threatening their marriage. It doesn't matter what 'mood' he is in, it always gets to him.

Which of the following would you recommend?

(a) He should somehow remove the trigger.

(b) He should alter his appraisal and judgement of the situation so that he sees it in a different way.

(c) The trouble is that he is displacing his anger inappropriately, not allowing it to leak away fast enough, or indulging in recreational anger. He should tackle this.

(d) He should work at strengthening his inhibitions, both moral and practical.

(e) He should alter his response to the situation, possibly by using the 'traffic lights' technique or by modelling himself on someone he knows.

(f) He should work on his beliefs, it is these that are really making him angry and irritable.

(g) He should work on his mood; sometimes he is in a good mood and sometimes he is in a bad mood and this is the real problem.

11 Brian has very serious problems with his anger; so much so that it sometimes lands him in front of the courts and indeed in prison. The most severe example is where he was drinking in a bar one night when a man next to him jogged his elbow so that Brian spilt beer down himself. Brian jumped to the conclusion that the man had done this deliberately to somehow show him up and make a fool of him. His anger was immediate and, without thinking, he smashed

his beer-mug against the bar and pushed the broken mug into the other man's face. Or at least, this is how he recollects it. He is now serving a five-year prison sentence.

Which of the following would you recommend?

(a) He should somehow remove the trigger.

(b) He should alter his appraisal and judgement of the situation so that he sees it in a different way.

(c) The trouble is that he is displacing his anger inappropriately, not allowing it to leak away fast enough, or indulging in recreational anger. He should tackle this.

(d) He should work at strengthening his inhibitions, both moral and practical.

(e) He should alter his response to the situation, possibly by using the 'traffic lights' technique or by modelling himself on someone he knows.

(f) He should work on his beliefs, it is these that are really making him angry and irritable.

(g) He should work on his mood; sometimes he is in a good mood and sometimes he is in a bad mood and this is the real problem.

12 Paul gets very frustrated in bringing up his 12-year-old son. He gives the example of how, recently, he found that the boy had lied to him about having done his homework: although he said he had done it, in fact he had not. This led to Paul impulsively hitting his son across the face and sending him to his room for the rest of the evening. It took them days to recover from this episode. Paul describes how sometimes he would take such an incident in his stride,

but other times he reacts angrily in this way. He thinks that the variation is sometimes caused by what has happened at work, in that when he has had a bad day he sometimes takes it out on his son. He also thinks there are times when he is just in a bad mood. In any event, he is very worried about the boy's future, with the result that if he doesn't do his homework Paul takes it very hard.

Which of the following would you recommend?

(a) He should somehow remove the trigger.

(b) He should alter his appraisal and judgement of the situation so that he sees it in a different way.

(c) The trouble is that he is displacing his anger inappropriately, not allowing it to leak away fast enough, or indulging in recreational anger. He should tackle this.

(d) He should work at strengthening his inhibitions, both moral and practical.

(e) He should alter his response to the situation, possibly by using the 'traffic lights' technique or by modelling himself on someone he knows.

(f) He should work on his beliefs, it is these that are really making him angry and irritable.

(g) He should work on his mood; sometimes he is in a good mood and sometimes he is in a bad mood and this is the real problem.

13 Tina has a problem with 'bouncers', doormen at night-clubs. She describes herself as a person who 'speaks her mind' generally, but with doormen it goes beyond that. She says that she doesn't really go looking for trouble, but

somehow or other she seems to repeatedly get into arguments with them. As a result she has been in numerous scuffles, and on three occasions it would be more accurate to say that Tina has assaulted the doormen in question. Rather strangely, perhaps, while she has assaulted three different doormen and been in scuffles with numerous others, she doesn't get into physical fights with anybody else.

Which of the following would you recommend?

(a) She should somehow remove the trigger.

(b) She should alter her appraisal and judgement of the situation so that she sees it in a different way.

(c) The trouble is that she is displacing her anger inappropriately, not allowing it to leak away fast enough, or indulging in recreational anger. She should tackle this.

(d) She should work at strengthening her inhibitions, both moral and practical.

(e) She should alter her response to the situation, possibly by using the 'traffic lights' technique or by modelling herself on someone she knows.

(f) She should work on her beliefs, it is these that are really making her angry and irritable.

(g) She should work on her mood; sometimes she is in a good mood and sometimes she is in a bad mood and this is the real problem.

14 Ken describes himself as 'stressed out'. He has what most people would regard as a high-powered job, and has somewhat more work than he can cope with. This leads to

him feeling bad during the day and, just occasionally, 'snapping people's heads off', as he puts it. However, what worries him most is how irritable he is back home. He feels sorry for his wife Trish having to live with him like this, but says that he cannot help it.

Which of the following would you recommend?

(a) He should somehow remove the trigger.

(b) He should alter his appraisal and judgement of the situation so that he sees it in a different way.

(c) The trouble is that he is displacing his anger inappropriately, not allowing it to leak away fast enough, or indulging in recreational anger. He should tackle this.

(d) He should work at strengthening his inhibitions, both moral and practical.

(e) He should alter his response to the situation, possibly by using the 'traffic lights' technique or by modelling himself on someone he knows.

(f) He should work on his beliefs, it is these that are really making him angry and irritable.

(g) He should work on his mood; sometimes he is in a good mood and sometimes he is in a bad mood and this is the real problem.

15 Chris says that he 'changes into a different person' when he gets in the car. From his account it would appear that he is responsible for 99 per cent of all of the nation's road rage incidents! Somebody only has to drive in a way that he takes exception to and his instant response is to tailgate or intimidate them. He knows this is wrong but 'cannot

help himself'. This is the only area that he has problems with.

Which of the following would you recommend?

(a) He should somehow remove the trigger.

(b) He should alter his appraisal and judgement of the situation so that he sees it in a different way.

(c) He is displacing his anger inappropriately, not allowing it to leak away fast enough, or indulging in recreational anger. He should tackle this.

(d) He should work at strengthening his inhibitions, both moral and practical.

(e) He should alter his response to the situation, possibly by using the 'traffic lights' technique or by modelling himself on someone he knows.

(f) He should work on his beliefs, it is these that are really making him angry and irritable.

(g) He should work on his mood; sometimes he is in a good mood and sometimes he is in a bad mood and this is the real problem.

Most of these cases are based on people I have seen in my professional capacity (with the notable exception of Danny and Vicky), so obviously I have changed their names and minor details (again with the exception of Danny and Vicky) to make them unidentifiable. I should stress that in the case of 'Danny and Vicky' I have no inside knowledge as to what irritates either of them or how they resolve matters between them.

The fact that I have seen most of the others professionally means that I feel I have 'the right answers'. It would be misleading to give these, however, because usually, there is more than one possible answer to the same problem. In fact, rather as a broken-down car is best pushed by several people, problems concerning irritability and anger are best tackled by means of several solutions. So it may be that, for a given case, a combination of two or more of the seven factors would work best.

So, ponder on some of these examples and discuss them with friends and relatives – who knows, you may produce the perfect answers!

PROJECT

Write out your own irritability/anger problem in a similar way to the fifteen examples given here. Then analyze it using the same seven questions (a)–(g). You now have your action plan!

Good Luck!

I hope you've enjoyed reading this book and, more to the point, I hope you have found it useful. I have certainly enjoyed writing it and confess to being pleased with the result. I think you have all the information here necessary to sort out your irritability or anger successfully and permanently.

Maybe, indeed, you have done so already, just in the course of your first reading. This is especially likely if you have chosen the projects carefully for yourself and implemented them thoroughly.

A word of caution and encouragement, however. Old habits die hard, and you may very well find that you have to reread parts of this book over months and even years to maintain your success. Indeed, I would urge you to do that, because the more pieces of the jigsaw you get in place, the easier it is to see a good clear picture. It may be that, when you first read through the book, you just 'cream off' the most relevant bits for yourself. On rereading you might implement other bits that are relevant, but not quite so relevant as the first level. This is still well worth doing, however, because it makes the whole process clearer and easier. So, do reread, lots of times if you want, because the projects are good ones and will really sort things out for you if you follow them through.

And one final thought: You probably embarked on this book out of consideration for those around you – and very commendable that is. Nevertheless, I hope you find that it has done wonders for your own enjoyment of life, too!

Appendix

Diary 1

Keep a record of when you get irritable or angry. Fill it in as soon as possible after the event. Note as clearly as possible what triggered your irritability/anger, and how you responded

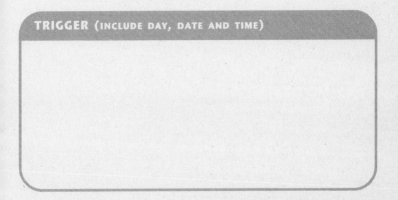

TRIGGER (INCLUDE DAY, DATE AND TIME)

RESPONSE (WHAT DID YOU DO?)

Diary 1: Fill in as soon as possible after the event

TRIGGER (INCLUDE DAY, DATE AND TIME)

RESPONSE (WHAT DID YOU DO?)

Diary 1: Fill in as soon as possible after the event

TRIGGER (INCLUDE DAY, DATE AND TIME)

RESPONSE (WHAT DID YOU DO?)

Diary 1: Fill in as soon as possible after the event

TRIGGER (INCLUDE DAY, DATE AND TIME)

RESPONSE (WHAT DID YOU DO?)

Diary 1: Fill in as soon as possible after the event

TRIGGER (include day, date and time)

RESPONSE (what did you do?)

Diary 2

Fill this in as soon as possible after each time you get irritable or angry

Trigger: Describe here what a video camera would have seen or heard. Include the day and date, but do not put what you thought or how you reacted.

Appraisal/Judgement: Write here the thoughts that went through your mind, as clearly as you can remember them.

Anger: Leave this blank for the time being.

Inhibitions: Leave this blank for the time being.

Response: Write here what a video camera would have seen you do and heard you say, as clearly as you can.

More helpful appraisal/judgement: How else might you have appraised the situation? To determine this, you might like to consider the following: What errors are you making (selective perception, mind-reading, awfulizing, emotive language, overgeneralization)?

If you had an all-knowing, all-wise friend, how would s/he have seen the situation?

Is a reframing of the situation possible? (A glass that is half empty is also half full.)

What would your cost–benefit analysis be of seeing the situation the way you did?

Diary 2

Fill this in as soon as possible after each time you get irritable or angry

Trigger: Describe here what a video camera would have seen or heard. Include the day and date, but do not put what you thought or how you reacted.

Appraisal/Judgement: Write here the thoughts that went through your mind, as clearly as you can remember them.

Anger: Leave this blank for the time being.

Inhibitions: Leave this blank for the time being.

Response: Write here what a video camera would have seen you do and heard you say, as clearly as you can.

More helpful appraisal/judgement: How else might you have appraised the situation? To determine this, you might like to consider the following: What errors are you making (selective perception, mind-reading, awfulizing, emotive language, overgeneralization)?

If you had an all-knowing, all-wise friend, how would s/he have seen the situation?

Is a reframing of the situation possible? (A glass that is half empty is also half full.)

What would your cost–benefit analysis be of seeing the situation the way you did?

Diary 2

Fill this in as soon as possible after each time you get irritable or angry

Trigger: Describe here what a video camera would have seen or heard. Include the day and date, but do not put what you thought or how you reacted.

Appraisal/Judgement: Write here the thoughts that went through your mind, as clearly as you can remember them.

Anger: Leave this blank for the time being.

Inhibitions: Leave this blank for the time being.

Response: Write here what a video camera would have seen you do and heard you say, as clearly as you can.

More helpful appraisal/judgement: How else might you have appraised the situation? To determine this, you might like to consider the following: What errors are you making (selective perception, mind-reading, awfulizing, emotive language, overgeneralization)?

If you had an all-knowing, all-wise friend, how would s/he have seen the situation?

Is a reframing of the situation possible? (A glass that is half empty is also half full.)

What would your cost–benefit analysis be of seeing the situation the way you did?

Useful Resources

Organizations

Great Britain

**British Association of Behavioural
and Cognitive Therapies (BABCP)**
The Globe Centre
PO Box 9
Accrington BB5 0XB

Tel: 01254 875 277
Email: babcp@babcp.com
Website: www.babcp.com

**British and Association for Counselling
and Psychotherapy (BACP)**
BACP House
15 St John's Business Park
Lutterworth
Leicestershire LE17 4HB

Tel: 0870 443 5252
Email: bacp@bacp.co.uk
Website: www.bacp.co.uk

MIND: The National Association for Mental Health
Granta House
15–19 Broadway
Stratford
London E15 4BQ

MindinfoLine: 0845 766 0163
Email: contact@mind.org.uk

USA

The Association for Behavioral and Cognitive Therapies (ABCT) (Formerly the Association for the Advancement of Behavior Therapy)
305 7th Avenue
16th Floor
New York NY 10001

Tel: 001 212 647 1890
Fax: 001 212 647 1865
Website: www.aabt.org

Institute for Behavior Therapy
104 East 40th Street
Suite 206
New York NY 10016

Tel: 001 212 692 9288
Fax: 001 212 692 9305

Online services

www.wrongdiagnosis.com/sym/irritability.htm

www.cwgsy.net/community/mindinfo/anger.htm

www.mentalhelp.net
Click on 'Read & Listen' and select 'Psychological Self Tools eBook'

www.moodjuice.scot.nhs.uk/anger.asp

www.ezinearticles.com
Select 'Self Improvement' from 'Article Categories' and then 'Anger Management' and look up article 'Self Help Anger Management' by John Sullivan.

Useful books

Clark, Lynn *SOS Help for Emotions: Managing Anxiety, Anger, and Depression*, Parents Press (2001).

Gentry, W. Doyle *Anger Management for Dummies*, John Wiley & Sons (2006).

Lener, Harriet Goldhor *The Dance of Anger: A Woman's Guide to Changing the Patterns of Intimate Relationships*, HarperCollins (2005).

Peurifoy, Reneau *Anger: Taming the Beast: A Step-by-Step Program for Managing Anger Calmly and Effectively*, Kodansha America (2007).

Index

Order further books in the *Overcoming* series

Qnty	Title	RRP	Offer price	Total
	Bulimia Nervosa and Binge-Eating	£9.99	£7.99	
	Overcoming Anger and Irritability	£9.99	£7.99	
	Overcoming Anorexia Nervosa	£9.99	£7.99	
	Overcoming Anxiety	£9.99	£7.99	
	Overcoming Anxiety Self-Help Course (3 parts)	£21.00	£15.00	
	Overcoming Bulimia Nervosa and Binge-Eating Self-Help Course (3 parts)	£21.00	£15.00	
	Overcoming Childhood Trauma	£9.99	£7.99	
	Overcoming Chronic Fatigue	£9.99	£7.99	
	Overcoming Chronic Pain	£9.99	£7.99	
	Overcoming Compulsive Gambling	£9.99	£7.99	
	Overcoming Depersonalizaton and Feelings of Unreality	£9.99	£9.99	
	Overcoming Depression	£9.99	£7.99	
	Overcoming Insomnia and Sleep Problems	£9.99	£7.99	
	Overcoming Low Self-Esteem	£9.99	£7.99	
	Overcoming Low Self-Esteem Self-Help Course (3 parts)	£21.00	£15.00	
	Overcoming Mood Swings	£9.99	£7.99	
	Overcoming Obsessive Compulsive Disorder	£9.99	£7.99	
	Overcoming Panic	£9.99	£7.99	
	Overcoming Panic and Agoraphobia Self-Help Course (3 parts)	£21.00	£15.00	
	Overcoming Paranoid and Suspicious Thoughts	£9.99	£7.99	
	Overcoming Problem Drinking	£9.99	£7.99	
	Overcoming Relationship Problems	£9.99	£7.99	
	Overcoming Sexual Problems	£9.99	£7.99	
	Overcoming Social Anxiety and Shyness Self-Help Course (3 parts)	£21.00	£15.00	
	Overcoming Traumatic Stress	£9.99	£7.99	
	Overcoming Weight Problems	£9.99	£7.99	
	Overcoming Worry	£9.99	£7.99	
	Overcoming Your Child's Fears and Worries	£9.99	£7.99	
	Overcoming Your Child's Shyness and Social Anxiety	£9.99	£7.99	
	Overcoming Your Smoking Habit	£9.99	£7.99	
	Manage Your Mood	£12.99	£10.99	
	P&P	**FREE**	**FREE**	
	TOTAL			

Name: _____

Address: _____

_____ Postcode: _____

Daytime Tel No: _____

Email: _____

(in case of query)

How to Pay:

1. **By telephone**: call the TBS order line on **01206 255 800** and quote **ANGER**. Phone lines are open between Monday–Friday, 8.30am–5.30pm.

2. **By post**: send a cheque for the full amount payable to TBS Ltd, or if paying by debit, credit or Switch card, fill in the details above and send the form to:
Freepost RLUL-SJGC-SGKJ. Cash Sales/Direct Mail Dept, The Book Service, Colchester Road, Frating, Colchester, CO7 7DW

Constable & Robinson Ltd (directly or via its agents) may mail or phone you about promotions or products
Tick box if you do not want these from us ☐ or our subsidiaries ☐